1000 Places Washington

1000 Things to Do, See, and Experience in
Washington State for the Intrepid Adventurer

April Borbon

Copyright © 2012 April Borbon

All rights reserved.

ISBN:147931286X
ISBN-13:9781479312863

DEDICATION

This book is dedicated to my wonderful (and patient!) husband Tomas. Here is the book you have been waiting for!

CONTENTS

1 The Rules   vi

2 1000 Places list   Page 8

3 Index by Number   Page 286

4 Index by Location   Page 319

THE CHALLENGE

Part scavenger hunt, part history lesson, part adventure—your challenge is to do, see, and/or experience these 1000 things in Washington state.

The Rules:

1. Complete each task in whichever order you choose (there is space for notes under each task to keep you organized).
2. Do a bit of research on each task so you will have some background information on each challenge.
3. Record your experience (include the date as well as your impression of the experience and a photo) in the manner of your choosing (website, blog, etc. which can be accessed by the public).
4. Email us a link to your website/blog which we will then post on our website to share with others who are completing the 1000 Places challenge.
5. Help publicize the challenge so even more people will join in on the fun (through your website, Facebook page, Twitter, etc. at #1000PlacesWA).
6. Complete all 1000 tasks.
7. Email us when you have completed all 1000 tasks and we will send you a cool reward (and maybe generate some publicity for your accomplishment as well!).
8. Be creative. There is more than one way to meet these challenges.
9. Be careful. Some of these tasks can be dangerous or downright deadly. Use caution, an experienced

guide when necessary, and common sense when completing these tasks.
10. Work around any of these tasks that could cause you permanent harm (ie: if you are a recovering alcoholic, visit the wineries, take your photos, and skip the tasting room. If you are allergic to strawberries and the task says pick and eat a strawberry, don't do it! Just take a picture of the u-pick field sign. If the most exercise you get on a daily basis is moving from your couch to your kitchen, be sure to build up to climbing to the top of a mountain or backpacking into a remote mountain range).
11. If there are some tasks that are impossible for you to do, come up with a creative way to check off the task (ie: if you are blind, have a friend take a photo of the scenic vista for you. If you are wheel-chair bound, send up a representative—like a gnome or a teddy bear—to the top of Mount Rainier. If you can't run a marathon, can you walk it?).
12. Finally, we tried to choose places that will be available forever but sometimes things happen and places close or are no longer accessible. If you see that any of these tasks are impossible to complete for one reason or another, please drop us an email and let us know—we will immediately post a substitute for the task on the website.

Our email: email@1000PlacesWashington.com
Our website: www.1000PlacesWashington.com

SPECTATOR SPORTS

We love our spectator sports in Washington State. Check out these opportunities to cheer on Washington's favorite teams.

1. Watch a Seattle Seahawks football game.

2. Watch a Seattle Mariners baseball game.

3. Watch one of Washington State's four Western Hockey League (WHL) ice hockey team games in action.

4. Watch a Seattle Storm WNBA basketball game.

5. Watch a Seattle Sounders MLS soccer game.

6. Watch a baseball game featuring one of Washington State's six minor league baseball teams.

7. Watch a game (sport of your choice) at one of Washington's many universities or colleges.

8. Watch a roller derby featuring one of Washington State's half dozen roller derby teams.

9. Watch a high school-level sporting event (sport of your choice).

10. Watch the professional sporting event of your choice in Washington State (NASCAR, golf, etc).

WASHINGTON AUTHORS

Washington State has an incredible array of best-selling authors. Maybe it's the weather that makes one want to curl up with—or write—a good book. In this case, check out what Washington's authors have to share with you!

11. Read a romance novel by prolific Port Orchard author Debbie Macomber.

12. Read a true crime novel by best-selling author Ann Rule of Seattle.

13. Read a thriller by Tacoma author John J. Nance.

14. Read a novel by best-selling author Gregg Olsen (you may want to read his book "Starvation Heights" which figures prominently in task #31).

15. Read a novel by Kirkland writer Richelle Mead, a best-selling author of teen fiction.

16. Read a novel by best-selling romance author Julia Quinn of Washington State.

17. Read a legal thriller by best-selling Washington author Steve Martini.

18. Read a psychological suspense novel by Washington author Elizabeth George.

19. Read a book by Washington author Patricia Briggs who writes best-selling fantasy fiction novels.

20. Read a novel by best-selling romance author Lisa Kleypas who resides in Washington State.

OUTDOOR SPORTS

If there is one thing that will get Washingtonians off the couch, it is the opportunity to participate in a wide range of outdoor sports, come rain or shine. Give these sports a try and see what we mean.

21. Go kayaking in one of the many waterways of Washington State.

22. Go skiing or snowboarding at one of Washington's renowned ski areas.

23. Go fishing in a river, lake, or stream in Washington State.

24. Go camping at any of the number of camping areas throughout Washington State.

25. Bicycle one of the many scenic roads or trails around Washington State.

26. Try shooting at one of the many indoor or outdoor shooting ranges in Washington State.

27. Ride a dirt bike or ATV on one of Washington's many off-road trails.

28. Go shell fishing for crabs, clams, shrimp, oysters, etc. at one of Washington State's many saltwater beaches.

29. Go horseback riding in Washington State (but not in Wilber, that's its own challenge #121).

30. Play golf at one of Washington State's many golf courses.

DEATHLY PLACES

It isn't all sunshine and light in the great state of Washington, we have our own list of not-so-nice places with not-so-nice histories. Check out these places where tragedies have occurred.

31. Visit Starvation Heights, the site of the notorious sanatorium where guests were starved to death in the name of health (see #14).

32. Visit the site of the Wah Mee Massacre in Seattle, one of the deadliest mass murders in Washington State.

33. Visit the site of the Lakewood Police massacre, a coffee shop where four police officers were gunned down in cold blood.

34. Visit the site of the Whitman Massacre where 13 settlers were killed by Indians in 1847.

35. Visit the place where Kurt Cobain, lead singer of the band Nirvana, committed suicide.

36. Visit the site of the Capital Hill Massacre in Seattle.

37. Visit the site of the Centralia Massacre which took place in 1919.

38. Visit the Aurora Bridge in Seattle—nicknamed "Suicide Bridge"—where more than 230 people have jumped to their deaths since it was built.

39. Visit the site of the Pang Warehouse Fire in Seattle where four firefighters lost their lives fighting the fire.

40. Visit the site of Washington State's worst mining disaster in Roslyn.

BRIDGES

There's nothing like an awe-inspiring bridge to demonstrate what amazing feats of engineering are possible when people put their minds to it. Enjoy these fabulous bridges in Washington State.

1000 Places Washington

41. Visit the Bridge of the Gods; learn about the ancient bridge and legend.

42. Visit the Tacoma Narrows Bridge and learn about 'Galloping Gertie'.

Tacoma

43. Visit the Evergreen Point Floating Bridge, the longest floating bridge on earth.

Seattle

44. Visit one of the remaining covered bridges in Washington State.

45. Visit the Deception Pass Bridge, one of the scenic wonders of Washington State.

46. Visit the High Steel Bridge, a unique bridge in Mason County.

47. Visit the Bridge of Glass pedestrian bridge in Tacoma; it's not a bridge like others featured here but interesting and unique nonetheless.

48. Visit the Interstate Bridge which connects Vancouver to Portland; it's on the National Register of Historic Places.

49. Visit the Wishkah River Bridge in Aberdeen; it's on the National Register of Historic Places.

50. Visit the Montlake Bridge in Seattle, the site of "opening day" for boating season in Washington State.

SEATTLE LANDMARKS

The Seattle skyline is world-famous. Check out these famous Seattle landmarks and learn why they are so important to the city.

51. Visit the Space Needle, built in 1962 for the World's Fair.

52. Visit Pike Place Market, one of the oldest continually operating farmer's markets in the United States.

53. Visit the Columbia Tower, the tallest building in Seattle.

54. Visit the famous Fremont Troll, located under the Aurora Bridge.

55. Visit downtown Seattle's popular Chinatown-International District.

56. Visit Pioneer Square which was once the heart of the city of Seattle.

57. Visit the Seattle Center and International Fountain, the site of the 1962 Century 21 Exposition.

58. Visit the Smith Tower, the oldest skyscraper in Seattle.

59. Visit Westlake Center, often referred to as Seattle's 'town square'.

60. Visit the unique Ye Olde Curiosity Shoppe on Seattle's waterfront.

PLACES FROM MOVIES AND TV

Film makers love the natural beauty of Washington. See how they have used locations around Washington State to enhance their shows by watching these popular movies and TV shows.

61. Watch the 'Twilight' series of movies which is set in Forks, WA.

62. Watch the movie 'Officer and a Gentleman' which features Ft Worden as a backdrop.

63. Watch the movie 'Sleepless in Seattle' which was set in Seattle.

64. Watch the TV show 'Northern Exposure' which uses Roslyn, WA to represent an Alaskan town.

65. Watch the TV show 'Twin Peaks' which was set in Snoqualmie and North Bend.

66. Watch the movie 'Disclosure' which was set on Bainbridge Island and Seattle.

67. Watch the TV show 'Grey's Anatomy' which is set in Seattle.

68. Watch the TV show 'Frasier' which was set in Seattle.

69. Watch the movie 'The Vanishing' which was set in Washington State.

70. Watch the movie 'Free Willy' which used the scenic San Juan Islands as a backdrop for filming.

WASHINGTON-BASED BUSINESSES

We will again have to hand it to the weather of our great state to inspire world-famous businesses (at least where coffee and outdoor gear are concerned). Check out these Washington-based businesses that are known throughout the world.

71. Visit the international headquarters of Weyerhaeuser, one of the largest pulp and paper companies in the world.

72. Visit the original Starbucks store at Pike Place Market.

73. Visit the REI flagship store in downtown Seattle.

74. Visit the Amazon.com corporate offices in Seattle.

75. Visit the Microsoft campus in Redmond.

76. Visit the first Costco warehouse in Seattle.

77. Visit the first Zumiez store at the Northgate Mall in Seattle.

78. Visit the Expedia corporate headquarters in Bellevue.

79. Visit the Jones Soda headquarters in Seattle.

80. Visit the Nordstrom flagship store in downtown Seattle.

CEMETERIES

Washington State has many unique and interesting cemeteries—check out these examples.

81. Visit the Tahoma National Cemetery, the only National Cemetery in Washington State.

82. Visit Lake View cemetery; find Bruce and Brandon Lee's graves.

83. Visit the St Francis Mission Calvary Cemetery in Toledo, the oldest cemetery in Washington State.

84. Visit Greenwood Memorial Cemetery and find Jimi Hendrix's grave.

85. Visit the Maltby Cemetery in Duval and find out about its haunted history.

1000 Places Washington

86. Visit the Spokane Falls Cemetery and find out about the 1000 steps.

87. Visit the Sylvana Graveyard; it's reported to be haunted!.

88. Visit the Civil War Cemetery (next to the Lake View Cemetery), the only Civil War cemetery in Washington State.

89. Visit the Chief Joseph Cemetery; see where Nez Perce Chieftain Chief Joseph is buried.

90. Visit the Walla Walla State Prison Cemetery, a historic resting place for people who died while in the prison.

MOUNTAINS

Washington State is famous for its mountains. No matter where you look, when you look towards the Cascade Range, you will see towering, snow-covered mountains that create a beautiful backdrop for many of our cities and towns.

91. Visit Mount St Helens, Washington State's famously active volcano.

92. Visit Mount Rainier, the most glaciated peak in the contiguous United States.

1000 Places Washington

93. Visit Mt Baker, one of the snowiest places in the world.

94. Visit Mt Adams, the second highest mountain in Washington State.

95. Visit the Olympic Mountains and experience its wide range of ecosystems.

96. Visit Glacier Peak, one of the most isolated volcanic mountains in Washington State. *North Cascades*

April Borbon

97. Visit Mt Walker, the only peak facing the Puget Sound.

Quilcene

98. Visit Mount Si and enjoy the hike to the summit.

99. Visit Desolation Peak and hike to its summit.

No. Cascades

100. Visit Green Mountain in Kitsap County and hike to its summit.

PREHISTORIC PLACES

Although Washington is fairly young as far as states go, there are enough prehistoric sites in the state to keep the amateur archeologist busy for quite a while. Check out these fascinating prehistoric places in Washington State.

101. Visit the fascinating Ginkgo Petrified Forest.

102. Check out the ancient pictographs at the Cliffside Painted Rocks in Yakima.

103. View the Granite Canyon Rock Art in Omak.

104. Visit the Marmes Rock Shelter, one of the first National Historic Landmarks in Washington State, at Palouse Falls.

Franklin County (handwritten)

105. View the Long Lake Pictographs in Tumtum.

106. View the 44 ancient pictographs on Wedding Rock at Lake Ozette.

107. View the primitive rock art at Horsethief Lake State Park in Bingen.

108. Check out the artifacts from Ozette Village at Neah Bay.

109. Visit the Marymoor Prehistoric Indian Site located in Redmond.

110. Visit the Manis Mastodon Site near Sequim.

GARDENS

If there is one thing that the combination of weather and fertile ground does well in Washington, it is to create beautiful blooms. Washington State has a breathtaking array of gardens and arboretums to wow even the most jaded plant lover.

111. Visit the Volunteer Park Conservatory which features a Victorian-style greenhouse and a half dozen different display gardens.

112. Visit the beautiful Hulda Klager Lilac Garden.

Woodland

113. Visit the 200-acre Washington Park Arboretum on the shores of Lake Washington.

Seattle

114. Visit the award winning Bloedel Reserve on Bainbridge Island.

1000 Places Washington

115. Visit the Meerkerk Rhododendron Gardens which feature more than 1500 species of rhododendrons.

Whidbey Is

116. Visit the Kubota Gardens, a beautiful Japanese garden which is now maintained as a public park.

117. Visit the Manito Park and Botanical Gardens in Spokane.

118. Visit the Wright Park Arboretum and Seymour Conservatory in Tacoma.

119. Visit the fascinating Rhododendron Species Foundation and Botanical Garden.

120. Visit the pretty Bellevue Botanical Garden in Bellevue.

BREAK A LAW

This is one of those sections with its own disclaimer: we aren't responsible for you getting arrested and we won't bail you out of jail or pay your fines! Approach this section at your own risk! Now that that's clear, some laws were just made to be broken...like these.

121. Ride an ugly horse in Wilbur (the law: it's illegal to ride an ugly horse in Wilbur).

1000 Places Washington

122. Shuck peanuts on the streets of Bremerton (the law: it's illegal to shuck peanuts on the streets of Bremerton).

123. Buy a TV on Sunday in Spokane (the law: it's illegal to buy a TV in Spokane on Sundays).

124. Drink and dance at the same time in Lynden (the law: it's illegal to drink and dance at the same time in Lynden).

125. Walk about in public when you have a cold (the law: it's illegal in Washington State to walk about in public when you have a cold).

126.   Buy meat on Sunday (the law: it's illegal in Washington State to buy meat of any kind on a Sunday).

127.   Pretend that your parents are rich (the law: it's illegal in Washington State to pretend that your parents are rich).

128.   Eat a lollipop (the law: lollipops are forbidden in Washington State).

129.   Carry a fishbowl—with water in it—on a bus in Seattle (the law: it's illegal to carry a fishbowl with water in it on a city bus in Seattle).

130. Destroy another person's beer bottle (the law: it's illegal in Washington State to destroy another person's beer bottle).

HOT SPRINGS

What better place to hang out when the weather turns cold and rainy than a nice, bubbling, hot springs? Washington State has nearly a dozen popular hot springs that will help you soak your cares away.

131. Visit the therapeutic Sol Duc Hot Springs on the Olympic Peninsula.

132. Enjoy the therapeutic mineral water at the Bonneville Hot Springs.

133. Relax in the therapeutic mineral waters of the Carson Hot Springs.

134. Visit the undeveloped Olympic Hot Springs on the Olympic Peninsula.

135. Take a short hike and visit the Baker Hot Springs.

136. Enjoy the Wind River Hot Springs which is adjacent to the Wind River.

137. Visit the remote Gamma Hot Springs located in the Glacier Peak Wilderness.

138. Visit the Scenic Hot Springs (note that access may be a bit of a challenge).

139. Visit the rustic Goldmyer Hot Springs.

140. Find the elusive Sulpher Hot Springs in the Glacier Peak Wilderness.

April Borbon

WATERFALLS

Waterfalls are awe-inspiring for both the beauty and power they display. Fortunately, Washington State has many such waterfalls that will take your breath away!

141. Visit Cedar Falls and learn about its long history.

142. Visit Feature Show Falls, one of the most beautiful waterfalls in the North Cascades.

143. Visit Wallace Falls—actually a series of nine falls—which are some of the tallest in the state.

1000 Places Washington

144. Visit the pretty Otter Falls located in King County.

145. Visit Twin Falls—both the Upper Falls and Middle Falls—at Olallie State Park.

146. Visit Franklin Falls located just off I-90.

147. Visit Sol Duc Falls in Clallam County, one of the most photographed falls in the state.

148. Visit Marymere Falls just west of Port Angeles.

149. Visit the beautiful Lower Falls Creek Falls.

150. Visit the Ancient Lake waterfalls which are fed from irrigation activity in the area.

GOVERNMENT

Of course you can't have a state without a bit of government. Check out these places and things that exemplify government in Washington State.

151. Visit Washington's State Capitol Campus in Olympia.

152. Visit a county courthouse in Washington State—there are 39 to choose from!

153. Sit in on a legislative session in Olympia and watch Washington State government in action.

154. Participate in a protest and watch freedom in action.

155. Learn about the Washington State caucus system that determines the presidential nominee for the state.

156. Meet a legislator from Washington State.

157. Attend an event at the Washington State Capitol Campus.

158. Take a photo of the Washington State Flag and learn about its history.

159. Take a photo of something that officially represents Washington State (state bird, state flower, etc).

160. Attend a political rally and watch another example of politics in action.

LEWIS AND CLARK

You can't be a school kid in Washington without learning about explorers Lewis and Clark who visited the state in 1805. Check out these places where they left their mark on Washington State history.

161. Visit Chief Timothy State Park and learn about Lewis and Clark's meeting with the Nez Perce Indians.

162. Visit Boyer Park and find the interpretive sign about the Lewis and Clark Expedition.

163. Visit Lyons Ferry State Park and find the interpretive sign about the Lewis and Clark Expedition.

164. Visit Sacajawea State Park and learn about the Lewis and Clark Expedition at the Interpretive Center.

165. Visit Horsethief Lake State Park where once stood an Indian village that Lewis and Clark stayed at during their journey.

166. Visit Fort Columbia State Park, an area visited by Lewis and Clark.

167. Visit the Lewis and Clark Trail State Park and find the interpretive sign about the explorers.

168. Visit Cape Disappointment State Park where Lewis and Clark reached the mouth of the Columbia River and visit the Interpretive Center.

169. Drive the Lewis and Clark Memorial Highway, also known as WA-14, a 176-mile drive from Vancouver to Plymouth.

170. Visit the Lewis and Clark State Park in Winlock; note that the park was named for the explorers even though they never visited the area.

WINERIES

It turns out that some areas of Washington State can rival the best grape-growing regions of the world. Check out these wineries that showcase delicious Washington-grown wine.

171. Take a tour of the Chateau Ste Michelle Winery in Woodinville.

172. Visit the Kiona Vineyards Winery in Benton City.

173. Visit the Gorman Winery in Woodinville.

174. Visit Two Mountain Winery and Vineyard in Zillah.

175. Tour the family-owned Hedges Cellars Winery in Benton City.

176. Tour the Fidelitas Winery in Benton City.

177. Visit the Col Salare Winery in Benton City.

178. Tour the Terra Blanca Winery and vineyard in Benton City.

179. Visit the Harbinger Winery in Port Angeles.

180. Visit the Olympic Cellars Winery near Port Angeles.

BREWERIES

Although Washington wines may compete on the world stage, our breweries aren't to be left behind. Craft brewing is all the rage in Washington State. Check out these Washington-based small breweries that have made a name for themselves around the country and around the world.

181. Visit the Boundary Bay Brewery, a winner of many brewing awards.

182. Visit the Pyramid Brewery's original location in Seattle.

183. Take a tour of the Elysian Brewing Company in Seattle.

184. Tour the Redhook Ale Brewery in Woodinville.

185. Tour the Iron Horse Brewery in Ellensburg.

186. Visit the Fish Tale Brew Pub in Olympia which is noted for its hand-crafted Northwest ales.

187. Visit the Pike Brewing Company in downtown Seattle.

188. Visit the Elliot Bay Brewing Company which consistently scores great reviews.

189. Visit the Black Raven Brewing Company in Redmond.

190. Tour the Icicle Brewing Company in Leavenworth.

ISLANDS

Washington State really does have a little bit of everything. One thing we love about the state is that it has a whole bunch of islands which add to the scenery and uniqueness of the state.

191. Visit Bainbridge Island which is a short ferry ride from downtown Seattle.

192. Visit any of the San Juan Islands (only four are reachable by ferry).

193. Visit McNeil Island which was one of the last remaining prison islands in the country when it closed.

194. Visit Blake Island and learn about its fascinating history.

195. Visit Vashon Island, one of the largest islands in Puget Sound.

196. Visit picturesque Whidbey Island, the largest island in Washington State.

197. Visit Harbor Island which was once the largest artificial island in the world.

198. Visit the quaint Lummi Island located in Whatcom County.

199. Visit Puget Island which is located in the Columbia River.

200. Visit Protection Island (this may not be as easy as it sounds!).

LAKES

Washington also has a whole bunch of lakes—deep lakes, shallow lakes, big lakes, small lakes. Check out this wide array of lakes and see for yourself.

1000 Places Washington

201. Visit Lake Crescent, possibly the deepest lake in Washington State.

202. Visit Lake Washington, the second largest natural lake in Washington State.

203. Visit Vancouver Lake—one of the shallower lakes in the state with a mean depth of only three feet!

204. Visit Lake Chelan; at 55 miles long it is the largest natural lake in the state.

205. Visit Lake Sammamish, a beautiful eight-mile long lake east of Seattle.

206. Visit Lake Roosevelt, the largest lake and reservoir in Washington State.

207. Visit Lake Ozette, located on the Olympic Peninsula.

208. Visit Moses Lake in Grant County, once called Salt Lake before being renamed.

209. Visit Soap Lake, a lake in which the naturally occurring foam and mineral-rich waters give the lake a soapy feel.

210. Visit Spirit Lake, once decimated by the eruption of Mt St Helens but now it is once again a popular tourist spot.

RIVERS

Our geology lesson would not be complete without visiting some of the amazing rivers in Washington State—from the longest to the shortest and other interesting rivers as well.

211. Visit the Columbia River, the longest river in Washington State.

212. Visit the Yakima River which irrigates the agricultural land of the Yakima Valley.

213. Visit the Snake River, the largest tributary of the Columbia River.

214. Visit the Wind River which is wholly contained in Skamania County.

215. Visit the White Salmon River which is designated as a Wild and Scenic River.

216. Visit the popular Stillaguamish River in northwestern Washington.

217. Visit the Sol Duc River on the Olympic Peninsula.

218. Visit the Snoqualmie River which is noted for flooding nearly every year.

219. Visit the Green River which has been infamously linked with the Green River Killer.

220. Visit the Chelan River, the shortest river in Washington State.

LIGHTHOUSES

What do you get when you have miles and miles of rugged coastline? Lighthouses, of course. Check out these often photographed lighthouses that are at once both practical and beautiful.

221. Visit the Point No Point Lighthouse, the oldest lighthouse on Puget Sound.

222. Visit the Cape Flattery Lighthouse, the lighthouse which is located the furthest north on the West Coast of the continental United States.

223. Hike out to the New Dungeness Lighthouse on the Dungeness Spit.

224. Visit the Mukilteo Lighthouse, one of the few lighthouses constructed entirely with wood.

225. Visit the Alki Point Lighthouse near downtown Seattle.

226. Visit the Admiralty Head Lighthouse, one of the earliest navigational aids in the West.

227. Visit the Grays Harbor Lighthouse, the tallest lighthouse in Washington State.

228. Visit the North Head Lighthouse; find out why it is one of two lighthouses at Cape Disappointment.

229. Visit the Browns Point Lighthouse which is on the National Register of Historic Places.

230. Visit the Cape Disappointment Lighthouse, the oldest lighthouse in the Pacific Northwest.

TAKE A SCENIC DRIVE

Sometimes you need do no more to see the beautiful scenery of Washington than drive down the road...as exemplified in these scenic drives around the state.

231. Drive the 367-mile stretch of Washington State's portion of Highway 101 from Olympia to the Oregon border.

232. Drive the 107-mile Chinook Pass Scenic Byway from Sumner to Naches.

233. Drive the beautiful 440-mile Cascade Loop Scenic Highway.

234. Drive the 330-mile Olympic Peninsula Loop which circles the entire Olympic Peninsula.

235. Drive the 52-mile Mountain Loop Highway (be warned, only part of it is paved!).

236. Drive the 69-mile Spokane River Loop and explore the varying scenery along the way.

237. Drive the 208-mile Palouse Scenic Byway.

238. Drive the 54-mile Whidbey Island Scenic Byway, the first designated Washington State Scenic Byway on an island.

239. Drive the scenic 21-mile route called Chuckanut Drive from Burlington to Bellingham.

240. Drive the 27-mile North Pend Oreille Scenic Byway in the "Forgotten Corner" of northeast Washington State.

DANGEROUS PLACES

First, again, the disclaimer: these places are DANGEROUS so do these tasks at your own risk. We aren't responsible for anything...unfortunate...that happens to you. Now, like any other state, Washington has places that are notably dangerous, but you may want to check them out just the same.

241. Drive down Interstate 5, the only highway in Washington to rank on the 'America's 100 Deadliest Highways' list; it was ranked #94.

242. Swim in the Pacific Ocean but be careful of riptides, one of the deadly hazards on Washington's coastal beaches.

243. Visit the "ghetto" area of a major Washington city—White Center, Skyway, Hilltop—there are a number of areas noted for gang violence in Washington State.

244. Visit the lahar zone around Mt Rainier and learn why this area is considered so dangerous.

245. Take a photo of your home...or someone else's home; a private home is statistically the most common place for people to die in Washington State.

246. Visit the mountains of Washington State; dangers here range from the mundane such as getting lost and dying from exposure to tangling with wildlife or even a volcano.

247. Visit the Washington coast and find out about the danger of tsunamis and what you should do if caught in such a situation.

248. Attend a DUI Victim's Panel and learn about the dangers of drinking and driving, a common cause of fatalities on Washington's roads.

249. Earthquakes are not uncommon in Washington State; find an area where earthquake damage has occurred.

250. Wildfires are also a common danger in Washington State; take a photo of recent wildfire damage somewhere in the state.

HIGHER LEARNING

Washington State has one of the most educated populations in the nation. We are assuming that is due, in large part, to the number of amazing institutions of higher learning that dot nearly all corners of the state.

251. Visit the University of Washington, the oldest university in Washington State.

252. Visit Washington State University, the state's largest land-grant university.

253. Visit the Evergreen State College, founded in 1967 to be an experimental, non-traditional college.

254. Visit Gonzaga University, a private, Roman Catholic university with a long list of successful graduates.

255. Visit Bastyr University, the largest accredited naturopathic medical school in the United States.

256. Visit the Art Institute of Seattle which provides a unique higher education in the creative arts.

257. Visit Cornish College of the Arts, a nationally-recognized college of the performing arts.

1000 Places Washington

258. Visit Seattle University, the largest independent university in the northwestern United States.

259. Visit one of the state universities (besides WSU and UW) located throughout the State of Washington—Eastern, Western, or Central Washington universities.

260. Visit a local community college; there are many to choose from throughout the state.

PERFORMING ARTS

Sometimes you just need to kick back, relax and be entertained. Washington State can provide that too! Enjoy these performing arts events and the talented performers who call Washington State home.

261. Watch the amazing Seattle Symphony perform.

262. Watch the renowned Pacific Northwest Ballet perform.

263. Attend an event at the Washington Center for the Performing Arts.

264. Watch a live community theater performance at one of the many community theaters in Washington State.

265. Watch a performance by the acclaimed Seattle Opera.

266. Watch a performing arts event put on by students at a college or university.

267. Attend an event at the Seattle Repertory Theater, the largest non-profit resident theater in the Pacific Northwest.

268. Attend a Spokane Symphony performance.

269. Attend a performance at the Performing Arts Center of Wenatchee.

270. Attend a performance by a local dance troupe (dance school recital, folk dance program, etc).

CASINOS

On the other hand, you may want to jump in on the action and what better way than to bet it all on black (or red, or odd, or even...you get the idea). Gambling is legal in Washington State and that has led to a profusion of casinos to meet your every wagering need.

271. Visit the Tulalip Casino, the largest casino in Washington State.

272. Visit the popular Muckleshoot Casino located in Auburn.

273. Visit the LaCenter casino complex; it is a short drive from I-5.

274. Visit the Seven Cedars Casino located on the Olympic Peninsula.

275. Visit the Suquamish Clearwater Casino, a destination resort on the Kitsap Peninsula.

276. Visit both parts of the Emerald Queen Casino located in Tacoma and Fife.

277. Visit the Snoqualmie Casino, one of the newest casinos in Washington State.

278. Visit the Quinault Casino located on the beautiful Washington coast.

279. Visit the Northern Quest Casino, a destination resort near Spokane.

280. Visit the Skagit Valley Casino, just off of I-5 in Bow.

SHOPPING

And then there is always shopping when you want to throw your money down on a sure thing. From the unique to the name brand to the high end to the odd, you are sure to find enough shopping in Washington State to satisfy all of your consumer needs.

281. Shop at one of the half dozen outlet malls in Washington State.

282. Buy something unique at Ye Olde Curiosity Shoppe, the odder the better.

283. Shop at Nordstrom, a Seattle institution.

284. Shop for locally-made goods at Pike Place Market.

285. Shop at Uwajamaya in Seattle, one of the largest Asian shopping complexes in Washington State.

1000 Places Washington

286. Shop at one of the many shopping malls in Washington State.

287. Buy something online from Amazon.com, a Seattle-based business.

288. Shop at one of the many farmer's markets located throughout the state of Washington.

289. Shop at one of the numerous antique stores in Washington State.

290. Shop local, buy something from a non-chain store.

JUST FOR KIDS

Whether you have kids or you are a kid at heart, check out these unique kid-friendly places that promise hours of fun and entertainment for the young.

291. Visit the fascinating Seattle Children's Museum.

292. Visit the interesting Children's Museum of Walla Walla.

293. Visit the Imagine Children's Museum.

294. Visit the gum wall at Pike Place Market...and leave a piece of gum.

295. Visit the Hands-On Children's Museum in Olympia.

296. Check out the fascinating Soundbridge at Benaroya Hall.

297. Attend a screening at the Seattle Children's Film Festival.

298. Visit the Three Rivers Children's Museum in Pasco.

299. Run through the Rain Wall at Westlake Park.

300. Enjoy a farm experience at the popular Remlinger Farm in Carnation.

FACTORY TOURS

Take a peek behind the scenes to see how your favorite Washington-made products are produced with these fascinating factory tours.

　　　301.　Take the Boehm's Candy factory tour.

　　　302.　Take the Seattle Times newspaper plant tour and watch how a newspaper is made.

　　　303.　Take a tour of the Washougal Mill and watch how wool is turned into a blanket.

304. Take the Darigold factory tour in eastern Washington.

305. Take the Franz Bakery tour and watch how all of the bakery products you love are made.

306. Take the Liberty Orchards tour and see how the popular Aplets and Cotlets are made.

307. Take the Boeing factory tour and watch how an airplane is put together.

308. Take the Tsue Chong Fortune Cookie factory tour (find out what happens to the "unfortunate cookies").

309. Take the Theo Chocolate factory tour in Seattle.

310. Take a tour of the Orondo Cider Works and watch cider being made.

HISTORY MUSEUMS

Washington State may be a fairly young state but it does have quite a bit of history. Check out these interesting museums and learn more about the history of Washington State.

311. Visit the Washington State History Museum and learn about Washington's history.

312. Visit the Burke Museum of Natural History and Culture, the oldest museum in Washington State.

313. Visit the Museum of History and Industry and learn about the history of Seattle and its environs.

314. Visit the Whatcom Museum of History and Art.

315. Visit the small Quilcene Historical Museum and learn about the history of the western Olympic Peninsula.

316. Visit the Clark County Historical Museum and learn about the history of the Vancouver area.

317. Visit the Yakima Valley Museum; learn about the history of the settlers, and the Native Americans, in the Yakima Valley.

318. Visit the History House of Greater Seattle which highlights the history of various Seattle neighborhoods.

319. Visit the Grant County Historical Museum and Village, a complex of more than 30 buildings that reflect the history of the Grant County area.

320. Visit the Pomeroy Living History Museum, an interactive recreation of a 1920s-era working farm.

ART MUSEUMS

After you've done your fair share of absorbing the history of the state, switch to the creative aspects of Washingtonians and check out the many and varied art museums the state offers.

321. Visit the Seattle Art Museum which is filled with wonderful collections and exhibits.

322. Visit the Seattle Asian Art Museum which has one of the largest collections of Asian art in the state.

323. Visit the Museum of Glass and watch how glass art is made.

324. Visit the Maryhill Museum of Art and enjoy its eclectic collection of artwork.

325. Visit the Henry Art Gallery, the first public art museum in the state of Washington.

326. Visit the Tacoma Art Museum and check out its interesting collections.

327. Visit the Museum of Northwest Art which focuses on the Northwest School art movement.

328. Visit the Frye Art Museum which focuses on paintings and sculptures from the 19th century forward.

329. Visit the Jundt Art Museum located on the campus of Gonzaga University.

330. Visit the Northwest Museum of Art and Culture, a unique museum which includes five underground galleries.

OTHER MUSEUMS

True to its nature, Washington State museums are not all about art and history. Check out these (often off-the-wall) museums that can be found around the state.

331. Visit the Science Fiction Museum and Hall of Fame, a unique museum that is the first of its kind in the world.

332. Visit Marvin Carr's One of a Kind in the World Museum which houses a little bit of everything.

333. Visit Marsh's Free Museum, a unique museum which features all kinds of curiosities.

334. Visit Camlann Medieval Village, a recreation of an English village, circa 1376!

335. Visit the Robot Hut Museum which features…robots!

336. Visit the Northwest Museum of Legends and Lore, a small, interesting, one-room museum.

337. Visit the Seattle Metropolitan Police Museum and learn about the history of law enforcement in the Seattle area.

338. Visit the Washington Banana Museum, a museum you visit online!

339. Visit the World Kite Museum, the only museum in America dedicated to kites.

340. Visit the Rosalie Whyel Museum of Doll Art, one of the premier doll museums in the world.

UNIQUE RESTAURANTS

It's impossible to list all of the great restaurants in Washington so here is a sample of what the state has to offer on the restaurant front—a selection of unique and interesting must-try restaurants.

341. Visit the Herb Farm Restaurant, an award-winning restaurant that focuses on preparing locally-grown food.

342. Visit the Seattle Space Needle Restaurant, a restaurant that rotates as you dine giving you a complete view of the city.

343. Have dim sum in Seattle's Chinatown and pick your lunch off of the carts as they roll by.

344. Visit the Chefs Kitchen at the Inn at Langley restaurant and enjoy a unique dining experience.

345. Visit the Ajax Café; don't forget to try on some of their hats.

346. Visit Molly Ward Gardens, a rural farmhouse restaurant in Poulsbo.

347. Visit Fat Smitty's Café; don't forget to leave a dollar on the wall while you are there.

348. Visit the Grant House, a popular restaurant situated on Vancouver's famous Officer's Row.

349. Take a dinner cruise on either the Columbia River or Puget Sound.

350. Visit the Chaco Canyon Café and enjoy a completely organic, vegetarian meal.

TAKE A HIKE

Instead of just looking at all of the beautiful scenery that abounds in Washington State, get out in it by taking a hike along these popular hiking corridors.

351. Hike the 14.7 mile Interurban Trail in King County.

352. Hike to the top of Beacon Rock, a short but steep trail that will lead to spectacular views of the Columbia River Gorge.

353. Hike the Clear Creek Trail from Silverdale's Waterfront Park to Trigger Avenue.

354. Hike the Hoh Rainforest Trail which will take you through the Hall of Mosses then on to the Hoh River.

355. Hike the Capitol Forest Trail located just outside of Olympia.

356. Hike the 11-mile long Paradise Valley Trail in Snohomish County.

357. Hike the Spruce Railroad Trail around Lake Crescent.

358. Hike the scenic Point of the Arches Trail on the northwestern coast of Washington State.

359. Hike the Snoqualmie Falls Trail, a short trail that will lead to a spectacular view of the falls.

360. Hike the 31-mile Klickitat Trail which follows an old railroad corridor to the Columbia River Gorge.

MILITARY

Due to its unique location and geography, Washington State has many military installations. Learn more about the military in Washington by checking out these interesting bits of military culture.

361. Visit the USS Turner Joy Naval Ship Museum, a floating museum ported in Bremerton.

362. Visit a military base; there are more than a dozen to choose from in Washington State.

363. Visit the Washington State Veteran's Memorials located on the State Capitol campus.

364. Visit the Naval Undersea Warfare Museum and learn how submarines were developed and used throughout naval history.

365. Visit the Fort Lewis Military Museum, a historical museum that houses a number of military artifacts.

366. Visit the Puget Sound Navy Museum and learn about the history of the US Navy.

367. Stop into a VFW Hall and thank a veteran for their service.

368. Visit the Eastern Washington State Veteran's Cemetery and see the graves of those who have served our country.

369. Visit a veteran at one of the three Washington State Veteran's Homes in the state and thank them for their service.

370. Watch a Veteran's Day parade; there are many held throughout the state each Veteran's Day.

AGRICULTURE

Washington State—particularly the eastern half of the state—is a world supplier of many types of produce and grains. Check out Washington's crops and sample many of these items fresh off the vine.

371. Eat apples grown in Washington, one of the state's premier crops.

372. Eat strawberries grown in Washington; pick them at a u-pick farm.

373. Eat cherries grown in Washington, another premier agricultural crop of the state.

374. Eat potatoes that were grown in Washington State.

375. Eat raspberries grown in Washington; pick them at a u-pick farm.

376. Eat grapes grown in Washington; pick them off the vine at a u-pick farm.

377. Eat peaches grown in Washington picked right off the tree.

378. Eat apricots grown in Washington picked right off the tree.

379. Eat pears grown in Washington picked right off the tree.

380. Pick hops, an important agricultural crop on Washington State (but don't eat them!).

FORAGING

Of course not all of the tasty delicacies grown in Washington State are planted by farmers, many, in fact, grow wild around the state. Try foraging for these delightful items that often grace our plates.

381. Forage for wild blackberries which grow wild in Washington State.

382. Forage for wild huckleberries which grow in the mountains of Washington State.

383. Forage for wild mushrooms (but don't eat them unless you know they are edible!).

384. Forage for wild apples which grow on abandoned trees around the state.

385. Forage for wild greens; there are many varieties that grow wild around the state.

386. Forage for wild nuts that grow on abandoned trees throughout the state.

387. Forage for truffles which grow wild in the western part of the state.

388. Forage for other wild berries that grow wild around the state (other than blackberries and huckleberries).

389. Forage for wild cattails, an important crop for the ancient Native Americans in the state.

390. Try dumpster diving, a not uncommon way to forage in Washington State.

ARCHITECTURE

Although Washington may not rival other states in quantity when it comes to unique or historic architecture, it does have some buildings that have been internationally noted for their design.

391. Visit the much-lauded King County Library in downtown Seattle.

392. Visit the Rainier Bank Tower, called "cyber-gothic" and "weird" by reviewers.

393. Visit the Storybook House in Olalla, a house that looks like it jumped right off the pages of a children's story book.

394. Visit Fort Nisqually and check out the architecture of this early fort built in Washington State.

395. Visit the Territorial Courthouse in Whatcom County, the first brick building built in Washington State.

396. Visit the Bigelow House in Olympia, one of the few surviving examples of Carpenter Gothic architecture in the state.

397. Visit Manresa Castle, an actual castle built high on a hill overlooking Port Townsend.

398. Visit Troll Haven, a unique castle complete with trolls and gargoyles in Gardiner.

399. Visit the beautiful St John's Cathedral in Spokane.

400. Take a photo of the Experience Music Project building, a modern style building with "voluptuously undulating musical form".

BEACHES

With a location on the Pacific Ocean, a canal, and a sound, Washington State has a myriad of great beaches. Check out this selection of popular/ breathtaking/ beautiful beaches in the state.

401. Visit Long Beach on the Pacific Coast.

1000 Places Washington

402. Visit the popular Alki Beach in West Seattle.

403. Visit Deception Pass State Park Beach, a pretty beach on the Strait of Juan de Fuca.

404. Visit Rialto Beach, one of the most popular beaches on the Olympic Peninsula.

405. Visit Dungeness Spit, a 5.5-mile long sand spit bounded by the Strait of Juan de Fuca.

406. Visit First, Second, and Third Beach near LaPush, three beaches which were popularized in the Twilight book series.

407. Visit the beautiful Obstruction Pass State Park Beach on Orcas Island.

408. Visit Westport/Greyland/Tokeland Beaches, a series of beaches on the Pacific nicknamed the Cranberry Coast.

409. Visit Ediz Hook, a three mile long sand spit near Port Angeles.

410. Visit one of the beaches on the Puget Sound/Hood Canal; there are many to choose from.

SPAS

What better way to relax after a day of touring than at a spa? Washington State has a number of popular spas to meet all of your relaxation needs.

411. Visit the Great Wolf Lodge which has activities for the entire family.

412. Relax at the Bonneville Hot Springs Spa.

413. Enjoy the many amenities at the Tulalip Resort and Spa.

414. Visit the rustic spa at the Alderbrook Resort located on the shores of Hood Canal.

415. Enjoy the many amenities of the Semiahmoo Resort and Spa.

416. Visit the Chrysalis Inn and Spa, a luxurious spa located on Bellingham Bay.

417. Visit the Willows Lodge, a northwest style lodge and spa in Woodinville.

418. Visit the beautiful Salish Lodge and Spa perched just above the Snoqualmie Falls.

419. Visit the Rosario Resort and Spa which is on the National Register of Historic Places.

420. Visit the Skamania Lodge, a mountain resort and spa located in the scenic Columbia River Gorge.

UNIQUE FOOD

Most of the food you will eat in Washington State won't be that far from ordinary but Washington does have a few items that are unique to the state.

421. Eat a geoduck, an unusual clam native to Washington's coasts.

422. Eat an Applet and a Cotlet, a unique confection made in Washington State.

423. Eat artisan-style cured meats at Salumi in Seattle.

424. Eat salmon, a staple in Washington State.

425. Eat a Walla Walla Sweet onion, a popular onion grown in Washington State.

426. Eat venison (aka deer) hunted in Washington State.

427. Eat a river trout which are plentiful in Washington State.

428. Eat chicken feet in Seattle's Chinatown, it's a Chinese delicacy.

429. Try a Washington-made cheese made by one of the state's artisanal cheese makers (except Beechers, that's #772).

430. Eat a razor clam dug from one of Washington's beaches.

WEIRD WASHINGTON

Sometimes Washingtonians just need to cut loose and let their weirdness out...as in these examples.

431. Visit Bob's Java Jive and take a photo of the world's biggest coffee pot.

432. Find the Toe Truck, an actual tow truck shaped like a toe (there are two, find one).

433. Visit the Spite House and find out how it came to be.

434. Take a photo of the Flower Shop Elephant in Seattle.

435. Photograph the Chiropractic Bigfoot in Federal Way.

436. Find the Fremont Rocket and take a photo of it.

437. Photograph the Bigfoot Statue at the North Fork Survivor's Gift Shop and learn about the history of bigfoot in Washington State.

438. Photograph the World's Largest Egg in Winlock.

439. View the Right-wing Uncle Sam Billboard along I-5 in Chehalis and take a photo of it.

440. Take a photo of the controversial Lenin Statue in Seattle's Fremont neighborhood.

CHURCHES AND RELIGIONS

While Washington State is noted to have the fewest church-going people of any state in the nation, it still has a wide array of churches and places of worship to check out.

441. Visit the Indian Shaker Church in Marysville which was founded by an Indian shaman.

442. Visit St Demetrios Greek Orthodox Church in Seattle which hosts a number of community events each year.

443. Visit the St James Cathedral in Seattle, the mother church for the Archdiocese of Seattle.

444. Visit the Claquato Church, located in the oldest standing building in the state of Washington.

445. Visit the Idriss Mosque, the largest Muslim Mosque in Washington State.

446. Visit the Overlake Christian Church, one of the largest mega churches in Washington State.

447. Visit the Leavenworth UMC church which participates in many festivals in the town of Leavenworth each year.

448. Visit the Hindu Temple and Cultural Center in Bothel.

449. Visit Temple Emanu-El in Spokane, the first Jewish synagogue in Washington State.

450. Visit the Columbia River Washington Temple, a huge LDS temple in Richland.

QUAINT TOWNS

Washington State does quaint very well. Perhaps it is the seaside vistas, the dab of historical flavor, and the neatness of a small town that make these quaint towns an interesting place to visit.

451. Visit Port Townsend which features Victorian buildings and numerous cultural events.

452. Visit Poulsbo, a small Scandinavian-themed town.

453. Visit Leavenworth, a Bavarian-themed village in the mountains east of Seattle.

454. Visit Port Gamble which was once a company town for a timber mill.

455. Visit Gig Harbor, a quaint boating town on the shores of Puget Sound.

456. Visit Sequim, a retirement community in the rain shadow of the Olympic Mountains.

457. Visit Langley, a small town on Whidbey Island which hosts a number of community and cultural events each year.

458. Visit LaConner which is listed on the National Register of Historic Places.

459. Visit Winthrop, an Old West-themed town in the North Cascades.

460. Visit Elbe, the smallest town in Washington State with a population of 29.

PARADES

Everyone loves a parade and to that end, Washington State has a range of parades for all occasions.

461. Watch the Seattle Pride Parade, an annual parade that celebrates the LGBT community.

462. Watch the Seafair Torchlight Parade, one of the largest events of Seafair.

463. Watch the Annual Armed Forces Day Parade in Bremerton, the longest-running Armed Forces Day parade in the United States.

464. Watch the Fremont Solstice Parade which is famous for its interesting floats and the Solstice Cyclists.

465. Watch the Daffodil Festival Grand Floral Parade which was started in 1936 and is famous for traveling through four cities in one day.

466. Watch the Apple Blossom Festival Parade, a parade which celebrates the importance of apples in Washington State.

467. Watch the Viking Fest Parade in downtown Poulsbo which celebrates the area's Scandinavian heritage.

468. Watch the Irrigation Festival Parade which began over 100 years ago to celebrate the irrigation system that brought water to this dry part of the state.

469. Watch the Selah Days Parade which was started by pioneers in the area many years ago.

470. Watch the Woodland Planter's Day Parade which replaced the annual automobile tour of Woodland's dikes.

ANIMALS

Washington State also has its fair share of animals—wild and on display—at these animal parks and sanctuaries.

471. Visit the Woodland Park Zoo which began as a small menagerie on a private estate.

472. Visit the Olympic Game Farm, a drive-thru farm which allows visitors to see a number of large game animals.

473. Visit the Seattle Aquarium which is perched on the edge of Puget Sound in downtown Seattle.

474. Visit the Northwest Trek Wildlife Park and take a tram tour though this free-range wildlife park.

475. Visit the Point Defiance Zoo and Aquarium located near Commencement Bay in Tacoma.

476. Visit Wolf Haven, one of the top wolf sanctuaries in the country.

477. Visit the Ridgefield National Wildlife Refuge which provides vital habitat for migrating waterfowl.

478. Visit the Umatilla National Wildlife Refuge which is popular with bird watchers.

479. Visit the Theler Wetlands in Belfair and walk the tidal wetlands which are popular with bird watchers.

480. Visit the Cougar Mountain Zoo, a small zoo which features a number of endangered species.

FAIRS

Summer may be short in Washington State but it is prime time for fair-going. Check out these popular fairs in Washington.

481. Go to the Northwest Washington Fair which has been running for over a hundred years.

482. Go to a county fair—there are many to choose from.

483. Go to the Evergreen State Fair in Monroe which draws over 400,000 visitors annually.

484. Go to the Puyallup Fair which is rated one of the top ten largest fairs in the United States.

485. Attend the Washington Midsummer Renaissance Fair complete with costumes, merchants, and games.

486. Attend the Central Washington State Fair and find out about its interesting history.

487. Attend the Washington State Science and Engineering Fair which features young scientists and engineers from around the state.

488. Attend a Washington Civil War Association event and enjoy the fair-like atmospheres of a Civil War reenactment.

489. Attend the Fremont Fair, a very quirky, very popular annual street fair.

490. Attend a harvest celebration; there are many held throughout the state in the fall.

FESTIVALS

Also very popular during the short summer months are festivals that celebrate a wide range of things—from flowers to grains to kites!

491. Visit the Lavender Festival in Sequim, a weekend festival that celebrates the lavender grown in the area.

492. Visit the Skagit Valley Tulip Festival, the largest festival in Washington State which celebrates the tulips grown in the area.

493. Visit the Washington State International Kite Festival, an amazing week-long festival which draws kite flyers from around the world.

494. Attend the National Lentil Festival in Pullman, the largest celebration of lentils in the United States.

495. Attend the Model Train Festival, a popular festival held each year in December.

496. Attend Bumbershoot, one of the largest arts and music festivals in the United States.

497. Attend the Wooden Boat Festival which includes boat tours, races, and demonstrations.

498. Attend the Seattle International Film Festival which is one of the largest in North America.

499. Attend Oktoberfest in Leavenworth, a popular beer festival held each year.

500. Attend the Northwest Native Arts Market and Festival which includes native arts and crafts, drumming, singing, and dancing.

VIRTUAL VISITS

In this section you don't even need to leave the comfort of your home to check off these items—simply hop online and gain a bit of insight into these various sites in Washington State.

    501.   Find a coastal webcam that will give you a live view of the Washington coast.

    502.   Check out the Bonneville fish cam and watch the fish on the fish ladder.

    503.   Find a university webcam and watch what's happening in real time.

504. Find a mountain webcam and check out the view of the mountains.

505. Find a ski area cam and check out what's happening on the slopes.

506. Find a traffic cam and watch the traffic in real time.

507. Check out a ferry cam and get a live look at the Puget Sound from the ferry.

508. Find a city cam and check out one of the many cities around the state with this technology.

509. Find a scenic webcam in Washington State.

510. Find a weather cam and watch the weather live online.

BOOKS SET IN WASHINGTON

Just like the many authors who reside in Washington State, books set in the state are also quite popular.

511. Read 'Weird Washington' by Jefferson Davis, Al Eufrasio, Mark Moran, and Mark Sceurman and find even more amazing places to visit in Washington.

512. Read 'Snow Falling on Cedars' by David Guterson, the award winning book set in the Puget Sound area.

513. Read 'The Egg and I' by Betty MacDonald, called "a beloved literary classic".

514. Read 'Reservation Blues', a classic novel by Sherman Alexie which is set on the Spokane Indian Reservation.

515. Read 'Breakfast at Sally's' by Richard LeMieux about a homeless man and his friends in Bremerton.

516. Read 'Desolation Angels' by Jack Kerouac about the time he spent as a fire lookout in the North Cascades.

517. Read the mega-hit book series 'Twilight' by author Stephenie Meyer.

518. Read the action adventure novel 'Ghost Canoe' by Will Hobbs which is set on the northwest coast of Washington State.

519. Read the novel 'Hotel on the Corner of Bitter and Sweet' by Jamie Ford which is set in Seattle.

520. Read 'Drugstore Cowboy' written by James Fogel; the book was later made into and award-winning movie.

GIVING BACK

You will take away many things from this challenge, but it is also a good idea to give back. Here's how:

521. Volunteer at a soup kitchen or homeless meal place in Washington State (there are many to choose from).

522. Shop at a thrift store which then uses its profits to help those in need (Goodwill, St Vincent de Paul, etc).

523. Make up a sign and give out "free hugs" on a busy street corner.

524. Volunteer to help out at a community event in one of the many communities in Washington State.

525. Do a random act of kindness for someone in Washington State.

526. Donate your time, money, or needed items to a non-profit organization in Washington State.

527. Participate in a charity fundraiser held in Washington State.

528. Donate food to a community food bank in Washington State.

529. Help someone in need in Washington State.

530. Pay for the person behind you at Starbucks and start a Starbucks "Cheer Chain".

INDIE/VINTAGE

Check out the unique indie/vintage vibe that permeates various places around Seattle and around the state.

531. Listen to an indie band; note that Seattle is renowned for its many venues that feature indie bands.

532. Read an indie newspaper (for example, the 'Real Change' newspaper sold by Seattle's homeless).

533. Attend the Seattle True Independent Film Festival which has become a showcase for regional filmmakers.

534. Visit the Fremont Vintage Mall—an entire shopping mall filled with vintage wares for sale.

535. Shop at a vintage clothing store which are located in many cities around the state.

536. Visit one of the many indie craft fairs or markets in Washington State.

537. Shop for vintage memorabilia—anything from old signs to old records to classic giftware.

538. Visit Jack's Country Store in Ocean Park, a general merchandise store which opened in 1885.

539. Attend the Sasquatch Music Festival which showcases indie rock bands.

540. Shop at an indie bookstore; although their numbers are declining Washingtonians still love these types of bookstores.

DINERS AND DRIVE-INS

There's nothing like an old fashioned diner or drive-in to bring back the nostalgia of years gone by.

541. Eat at Beth's Café, famous for its 12-egg omelets.

542. Watch a movie at one of the few remaining drive-in movie theaters in the state.

543. Go to Dicks Drive In, a Seattle classic.

544. Go to Burgerville, a small drive-in chain based in Vancouver.

545. Go to Mike's Chili Parlor which was featured on the Food Network show 'Diners, Drive-Ins, and Dives'.

546. Go to Gee Cee's Restaurant, a well-known truck stop just off of I-5.

547. Visit the Southern Kitchen in Tacoma for some down-home southern cooking

548. Go to Voula's Offshore Café, another Washington restaurant featured on 'Diners, Drive-Ins, and Dives'.

549. Go to the Cougar Country Drive In, a family-owned drive-in restaurant in Pullman.

550. Go to the Big Apple Diner, a classic '50s style diner in Bremerton.

GROUP ACTIVITIES

Come and meet the locals by joining in on a group activity.

551. Go on a Volksmarch and explore the hidden areas of Washington State on foot with this popular group.

552. Attend one of the many HAM (radio) fests in the state.

553. Participate in a club event by joining up for an activity with a local biking, hiking, kayaking, skiing, etc. club.

554. Attend a bookstore event such as a book signing, story time, or other event hosted by your local bookstore.

555. Attend a meet-up with one of the many meet-up groups in Washington State.

556. Check out one of the many community gardens in Washington State.

557. Attend a community event (for ideas check out your local newspaper's community calendar).

558. Watch a kid's sports event which take place nearly every weekend around the state (soccer, Little League, etc).

559. Play a pick-up game of basketball or baseball in Washington State.

560. Attend an event to support your favorite political or social cause.

RACY THINGS

Yes, Washington State does have a bit of a wild side...

561. Visit a Strip Club (note that Washington laws are fairly restrictive so there is no alcohol served in these clubs).

562. Go to Emerald Downs—a horse race-y place in Auburn.

563. Bust out a song at a karaoke bar.

564. Participate with the Solstice Cyclists (which includes stripping off your clothes, painting your body, hopping on your bicycle, and joining the parade).

565. Visit a nude beach in Washington State.

566. Go gambling at one of Washington State's many casinos.

567. Crash a beach party on one of Washington's many beaches.

568. Visit the Rubber Rainbow Condom Company, a Seattle landmark.

569. Kiss Rachel the Pig at Pike Place Market.

570. Visit the Center for Sex Positive Culture and check out at public event at this, um, unique organization.

FAMOUS PEOPLE

Washington State has its share of amazing, creative, famous, and interesting people…

571. Listen to music by Washington-born Kenny G, an award-winning saxophonist.

572. Use software developed by Washington-born Bill Gates, the founder of Microsoft.

573. Listen to music by Sir Mix A Lot, a popular rapper from Seattle.

574. Read a hilarious 'Far Side' comic by Washington-born cartoonist Gary Larson.

575. View art work by famous glass sculptor and Washington-born artist Dale Chihuly.

576. Photograph something that represents Washington-born Olympic gold medalist Apolo Ohno.

577. Listen to music by Washington-born singer/songwriter Kenny Loggins.

578. Photograph something that represents Washington-born Randy Couture, a UFC champion.

579. Watch a movie featuring Washington-born actress Francis Farmer.

580. Watch a movie starring Bing Crosby, a famous Washington-born singer and actor.

INFAMOUS PEOPLE

...*Not to mention some infamous people as well.*

581. Learn about infamous hijacker DB Cooper.

582. Learn about infamous Green River Killer Gary Ridgway.

583. Learn about infamous serial killer Robert Lee Yates.

584. Learn about infamous serial killer Ted Bundy.

585. Learn about the scandalous burlesque dancer Gypsy Rose Lee.

586. Learn about Mary Kay Letourneau, the infamous Washington elementary school teacher who made headlines around the world.

587. Learn about how former Seattle Mayor Greg Nickels will be forever infamously linked with homeless encampments in Seattle.

588. Learn about infamous Aberdeen serial killer Billy Gohl.

589. Learn about "Barefoot Bandit" Colton Harris Moore.

590. Learn about the infamous Victor Smith and the lost treasure.

NATIVE AMERICAN TRIBES

With 29 federally-recognized tribes in Washington State, Native American culture is part and parcel of living in Washington. Learn more about these tribes.

591. Visit the Colville Tribal Museum and learn about the history of the Colville Tribe.

592. Visit the Yakima Nation Museum and Cultural Center and learn about the history of the Yakima Tribe.

593. Visit the Tulalip Tribe's Hibulb Cultural Center and learn about the history of the Tulalip Tribe.

594. Visit the Squaxin Tribe Museum, Library, and Research Center.

595. Visit the Makah Cultural and Research Center located at Neah Bay.

596. Visit the Suquamish Tribe Museum and learn about the history of this tribe.

597. Visit the Duwamish Tribe's Longhouse and Cultural Center and learn about the history of this tribe.

598. Visit the Steilacoom Tribal Museum and Cultural Center.

599. Visit the Puyallup Tribal Museum and learn about the history of the Puyallup Tribe.

600. Visit the Daybreak Star Cultural Center which represents all of the tribes of Washington State.

SCIENCE & TECHNOLOGY

Home to a bunch of high-tech companies and talented engineers, Washington State definitely has a big sci-tech culture.

601. Visit the Pacific Science Center, a fascinating museum that focuses on science, math, and technology.

602. Visit the Columbia River Exhibition of History, Science, and Technology, a museum and science center.

603. Tour the Hanford B Reactor and learn about the history of nuclear science in Washington State.

604. Visit the Future of Flight Aviation Center, an aviation museum and education center.

605. Visit the Museum of Flight and learn about the history of aviation in Washington State.

606. Visit the Goldendale Observatory and learn about astronomy.

607. Visit the LIGO Hanford Observatory and learn about this unique facility.

608. Attend one of the monthly "star parties" at the Jewett Observatory at Washington State University.

609. Visit the Jacobson Observatory and attend one of the public events at this facility at the University of Washington.

610. Visit the SPARK Museum of Electrical Invention and learn about radio, electricity, and other inventions.

MONUMENTS

Monuments to various causes can be found throughout the state of Washington.

611. Visit the Wild Horses Monument, an unusual piece of outdoor art on a bluff above I-90.

612. Visit the Fallen Firefighters Memorial and learn about the firefighters who died fighting the Pang Warehouse fire which inspired this memorial.

613. Visit the Peace Arch at the Washington-Canada border.

614. Visit Washington's own Stonehenge at Maryhill, the first monument in the United States to honor the dead of World War I.

1000 Places Washington

615. Visit the Gospodor Monuments, a controversial set of monuments long I-5.

616. Visit the Seattle Fisherman's Memorial which commemorates the many people in the fishing industry who have lost their lives to the sea.

617. Visit the George Washington Monument on the grounds of the University of Washington.

618. Visit the Bainbridge Island Japanese Exclusion Memorial which commemorates the internment of Japanese-Americans during World War II.

619. Photograph the Anderson Memorial which honors Columbia Astronaut Michael Anderson.

620. Visit the Bellingham Fisherman's Memorial which memorializes fishermen who have lost their lives at sea.

ANNUAL EVENTS

There are many annual events in Washington State that people look forward to all year, including these.

621. Attend the Scottish Highland Games which celebrate Scottish culture.

622. Go to Seafair, one of the largest summer events in Washington State.

623. Attend New Year's at the Needle, a popular way to ring in the new year.

624. Attend the Seattle Boat Show and check out what's new on the water.

625. Watch fireworks on the 4th of July at one of the many venues around Washington State.

626. Attend the annual Chinese New Year Celebration held each year in Seattle's Chinatown.

627. Watch the Christmas Tree Lighting in Leavenworth, a very popular annual festival.

628. Attend the Seattle Hemp Fest, a festival which draws over 200,000 people annually.

629. Go to one of the many haunted houses that spring up each fall to celebrate Halloween.

630. Check out one of the many annual Christmas Lighted Boat parades which take place on the water each December.

ETHNIC ENCLAVES

Washington State has a foreign-born population of more than 10% and in some areas you can hear more than 50 different languages spoken!

631. Attend one of the many Seattle Center 'Festal' cultural events that celebrate various ethnic heritages.

632. Go shopping in Seattle's Chinatown and see all of the unique and interesting items imported from Asia.

633. Attend a Dia de Los Muertos event held at various places around the state to celebrate this important Hispanic holiday.

634. Visit the Great Wall Mall, an Asian-themed mall in Kent.

635. Visit a Halal Market which caters to the needs of the state's Muslim population.

636. Visit a Filipino restaurant and learn more about this fascinating culture.

637. Attend a Hispanic music event; there are many held throughout the state each year.

638. Have a bowl of pho and enjoy a taste of Vietnamese culture.

639. Go to an Indian buffet and learn about popular dishes in the Indian culture.

640. Go to a Russian restaurant and experience the food of this large immigrant population in Washington State.

NATIVE AMERICAN CULTURE

Soak up some of the Native American culture which is prevalent in Washington State by participating in these cultural activities.

641. Watch the annual Tribal Journeys canoe event which takes place each summer along the shores of the Puget Sound and the Strait of Juan de Fuca.

642. Attend the Lelooska Foundation Living History Program show.

643. Experience the Tillicum Village Indian history program, a fascinating cultural experience on Blake Island.

644. Visit the Northwest Indian College which is located in Bellingham.

645. Attend the Omak Stampede Indian Encampment and Pow Wow, a popular annual event in Eastern Washington.

646. Attend the Annual Yakima Nation Treaty Days celebration which includes a rodeo and parade among other events that celebrate Native American culture.

647. Attend Makah Days, an annual event which includes dancing, singing, feasting, and canoe races.

648. Attend the Tulalip Annual Veteran's Pow Wow which celebrates the service of military veterans.

649. Attend Chief Seattle Days, an annual event that includes a salmon bake, canoe races, and a memorial honoring Chief Seattle.

650. Attend the Colville Tribe Annual Pow Wow, the Colville Tribe's largest yearly cultural event.

NATIONAL PARKS AND FORESTS

Washington State is home to a number of amazingly beautiful national parks and forests.

651. Visit Olympic National Park which includes coastlines, rain forests, and glaciers.

652. Visit Mt Rainer National Park, the fifth National Park established in the United States.

653. Visit the North Cascades National Park, one of the most wild and rugged national parks in Washington State.

654. Visit the Mount Baker-Snoqualmie National Forest which is the second most-visited national forest in the United States.

655. Visit the Gifford Pinchot National Forest, one of the older national forests in the United States.

656. Visit the Umatilla National Forest which features old-growth forest, mining, and a variety of wildlife.

657. Visit the Okanogan National Forest, the second largest national forest in the US that is contained within one county.

658. Visit the Wenatchee National Forest which features a little bit for everyone—hikers, climbers, fishermen, etc.

659. Visit the Colville National Forest which includes the last remaining herd of caribou in the contiguous United States.

660. Visit the Kaniksu National Forest, a small national forest in the northeastern portion of Washington State which was named after the black robes worn by Jesuit Missionaries who settled in the area.

THEATERS

Enjoy a bit of culture and entertainment at these popular theaters.

661. Visit Seattle's Cinerama Theater, one of only three remaining theaters still capable of showing three-panel Cinerama films.

662. Attend an event at the Intiman Theater, dubbed 'Seattle's classic theater'.

663. Visit the Broadway Center for the Performing Arts which is actually a complex of three theaters in Tacoma's historic theater district.

664. Visit the Capital Playhouse, an arts, education, and musical theater performance space in Olympia.

665. Visit the Marysville Opera House which is listed on the National Register of Historic Places.

666. Visit the Capitol Theater in Yakima, the primary performing arts facility in the region.

667. Visit the Moore Theater, the oldest still-active theater in Seattle.

668. Visit the Raymond Theater which features a theater Wurlitzer organ.

669. Visit the Ruby Theater in Chelan, one of the oldest movie theaters in Washington State.

670. Visit the Paramount Theater which was originally built to show silent movies and vaudeville performances.

STATE PARKS

Washington State has too many state parks to list. Here are some of the highlights.

671. Visit Lime Kiln Point State Park on San Juan Island which is one of the best land-based opportunities to see Orcas in the wild.

672. Visit Flaming Geyser State Park and learn about the underground methane pocket that keeps a continuous flame lit at the park.

673. Visit Bridle Trails State Park, a popular park for horseback riding and equestrian events.

674. Visit Dosewallips State Park which includes more than 5,000 feet of shoreline on the Hood Canal.

675. Visit Saint Edward State Park in Kenmore which was originally home to a seminary.

676. Visit Saltwater State Park which offers saltwater beaches on Puget Sound.

677. Visit Lake Wenatchee State Park which offers a number of outdoor recreation opportunities.

678. Visit Camano Island State Park which is located on the shore of Camano Island.

679. Visit Fay Bainbridge State Park which offers sweeping views of the Puget Sound and surrounding mountains.

680. Visit Potholes State Park, located on a series of lakes known as "potholes".

ADVENTURE SPORTS

Nothing like getting your blood pumping with these challenging adventure sports!

681. Go skydiving and check out the beautiful scenery of Washington State from above.

682. Go SCUBA diving at one of the many diving areas in the state.

683. Go bungie jumping at one of the places that offers this unique tourist attraction.

684. Go river rafting on one of Washington's many rivers.

685. Go rock climbing at one of the many popular climbing spots in the state.

686. Explore the Big Four Ice Caves, a unique set of ice caves in the Cascades.

687. Explore the Ape Cave, the longest continual lava cave in the continental United States.

688. Play paintball at one of the many paintball facilities in the state.

689. Go mountain climbing on one of Washington's many mountains (except for Mount Rainier which is its own challenge #802). Note: take an experienced guide with you if needed!

690. Do one of the many "tough man" races held in Washington State (Tough Mudder, Spartan Race, etc).

GREAT VISTAS

Washington State has a number of beautiful vistas to make you say "wow".

    691.   Take a picture of the beautiful Columbia River Gorge from the top of Beacon Rock.

[handwritten: Southern Cascades]

    692.   Take a picture of Puget Sound from high up in Seattle (from the top of the Space Needle, Columbia Tower, etc).

    693.   Take a picture of the rugged Washington Coast.

1000 Places Washington

694. Take a picture of the much photographed Hall of Mosses in the Hoh Rain Forest.

695. Take a picture from the top of Hurricane Ridge.

696. Take a picture of the amazing vistas of the Palouse.

Spokane

697. Take a picture from the mountain top of your choice.

698. Take a picture of the unique Channeled Scablands in Lincoln County.

699. Take a photo of fall foliage which can rival that of the northeastern US (along Hwy 101 on the Olympic Peninsula is a great place to do this!).

700. Take a photo of a mountain—there are an amazing variety of mountains in Washington State.

IN THE WATER

Washington State has a lot of water, and we aren't talking rain. Enjoy these water sports in the state.

701. Go swimming in a Washington State lake.

702. Slide down the Denny Creek slide, a natural rock waterslide at Denny Creek.

703. Snorkel or SCUBA dive at the Edmonds Underwater Park.

704. Body surf in the Pacific Ocean at one of Washington's coastal beaches.

705. Do the Polar Bear Plunge to celebrate New Year's Day at one of the many venues for this activity.

706. Go swimming in a Washington State river.

707. Visit one of the half dozen waterparks in Washington State.

708. Play in a tidal pool at a Washington State beach (watch for rogue waves!).

709. Go windsurfing in either the Puget Sound or Columbia River Gorge.

710. Go swimming in the Puget Sound or Hood Canal.

NIGHTLIFE

Your day isn't complete without a bit of nightlife, here's a selection of nightlife to enjoy in Washington State.

711. Go dancing at one of the many nightclubs in Washington State.

712. Go to a bar in the town of your choice.

713. Go to a movie at one of the many movie theaters in the state.

714. Kick up your heels at a square dance.

715. Attend a rave in Seattle.

716. Go to a comedy club in one of Washington State's bigger cities that offer this form of entertainment.

717. Watch a live band play at a bar or nightclub.

718. Watch a midnight movie at a movie theater (costume optional).

719. Play billiards at a bar or pool hall.

720. Go to a blues or jazz club and watch this interesting form of live music.

SEATTLE NEIGHBORHOODS

Seattle has dozens of neighborhoods, all with their own unique culture. Here are some of the most popular neighborhoods around the city.

721. Visit the Queen Anne neighborhood situated on the highest hill in Seattle and featuring Queen Anne-style architecture.

722. Visit the Belltown neighborhood, a trendy neighborhood located on the downtown waterfront.

723. Visit the Fremont neighborhood which was once the heart of Seattle's counterculture.

724. Visit the Ballard neighborhood, known for its heavy influence of Scandinavian culture.

725. Visit the Mercer Island neighborhood, considered the wealthiest neighborhood in Washington State.

Seattle

726. Visit the culturally diverse Beacon Hill neighborhood, home to many of the city's immigrants.

727. Visit the South Lake Union neighborhood which includes houseboats, industrial buildings, and commercial buildings located on the waterfront of Lake Union.

728. Visit the Wallingford neighborhood which is a mix of housing, public spaces, and business districts.

729. Visit the Capital Hill neighborhood which is the heart of Seattle's gay community and has a vibrant nightlife and entertainment district.

730. Visit the University District, a vibrant community which surrounds the University of Washington's main campus.

MODES OF TRANSPORT

Try these various modes of transport as you make your way around the state.

731. Take the Amtrak Coast Starlight train which runs the length of Washington State.

732. Take the Seattle monorail which runs through downtown Seattle.

733. Take the Seattle Link Lightrail which runs the length of the city.

734. Take a ride on a Washington State ferry; it is the largest ferry system in the US.

735. Take a city bus in one of Washington's cities or towns.

736. Take a seaplane ride which is often used for island hopping.

737. Take a ride on a private boat which are often used for pleasure and transport in Washington State.

738. Take a ride on the Seattle Sounder train which runs from Everett to Tacoma.

739. Fly in an airplane (preferably a Boeing).

740. Go canoeing, a form of transportation that was used by the Native Americans in centuries past.

PARTY CRASHING

Whether you are invited or invite yourself, check out these popular gatherings in Washington State.

741. Attend a convention in Washington State.

742. Participate in a flashmob—or form your own.

743. Participate in a cashmob—or form your own (this is a great way to support local businesses!).

744. Crash a wedding in Washington State.

745. Attend a college or high school graduation in Washington State and join in on the celebration.

746. Attend a Reddit meet up in one of the major cities of Washington State.

747. Crash a barbecue—whether in a park or in your own back yard.

748. Attend a Halloween costume party (costume required).

749. Attend an art show or gallery opening.

750. Attend a book club meeting in Washington State.

HOBBIES

Enjoy these popular hobbies while in Washington State.

751. Go bird watching and identify the birds you see.

752. Go rock hounding and identify some of the rocks you find.

753. Go fossil hunting in one of the locations around the state known for fossils.

754. Collect seashells from any of Washington's many beaches.

755. Go geocaching—find a geocache in Washington State.

756. Go metal detecting and see what interesting things you find.

757. Collect some beautiful flowers in Washington State and press them.

758. Collect some leaves in Washington State and identify them.

759. Go stargazing and identify some of the constellations you can see from Washington State.

760. Create a scrapbook of your adventures in Washington State.

COFFEE AND TEA

Washington State is synonymous with coffee, and we love our tea as well. Enjoy a cup at these popular places.

761. Visit a Starbucks coffee shop in Washington State (except for the original store, that's its own challenge #72).

762. Visit a Tully's Coffee shop, another popular coffee shop in Washington State.

763. Enjoy high tea at one of the many places that offer high tea service in Washington State.

764. Visit a BigFoot Java coffee shop, another popular Washington-based business.

765. Visit a Seattle's Best coffee shop, a business founded in Seattle in the 1970s.

766. Get your favorite beverage from a drive-thru coffee shop that features the controversial "bikini baristas".

767. Pick up your favorite beverage from a non-chain, local coffee drive-thru.

768. Buy coffee from a Washington-State small-batch coffee roaster.

769. Visit the tasting room at Seattle Coffee Works.

770. Get some coffee from the "Free Coffee Program" at one of Washington State's 26 highway rest areas that offer this program (don't forget to leave a small donation).

QUICK BITES AT PIKE PLACE MARKET

Pike Place Market is a foodie haven; try these quick samples of popular snacks while at the market.

771. Get a crumpet from the Crumpet Shop.

772. Try cheese from Beecher's Handmade Cheese Shop.

773. Enjoy a piroshky from Piroshky Piroshky.

774. Try donuts from the Daily Dozen Donut Company.

Seattle

775. Pick up a hom bao at Mee Sum Pastries.

776. Try smoked salmon from Pure Foods Fish.

777. Pick up some freshly made French bread from LePanier.

778. Try a freshly steamed tamale from El Puerco Lloron.

779. Have a pastry from Three Girls Bakery.

780. Try fish and chips from Jack's Fish Spot.

Seattle

DISTANCE TRAILS

These trails will definitely be a challenge as they are some of the longest in the state!

781. Hike the Washington portion of the Pacific Crest Trail.

782. Hike/bike the Mountain to Sound Greenway through the Central Cascades.

783. Hike/bike the 300-mile John Wayne Pioneer Trail.

784. Hike/bike the 27-mile Burke Gilman Trail.

785. Hike/bike the 126-mile Olympic Discovery Trail on the Olympic Peninsula.

786. Hike the 93-mile Wonderland Trail around Mount Rainier.

787. Hike/bike the 29-mile Snoqualmie Valley Regional Trail.

788. Hike/bike the 37-mile Centennial Trail near Spokane.

789. Hike/bike the Tolt Pipeline Trail in the Central Cascades.

790. Hike/bike the 15-mile Snohomish County Interurban Trail.

AMAZING STRUCTURES

Take a look at these amazing structures built in Washington State.

791. Visit the Bonneville Dam which was built to harness the Columbia River and generate power for the region.

Done

792. Visit the Grand Coulee Dam which was built to provide electricity and irrigation for the region.

793. Visit the Lake Washington Ship Canal/Chittenden Locks which connects Lake Washington to the Puget Sound.

794. Visit Tacoma's Union Station which features Beaux Arts architecture and a 90-foot high central dome.

795. Visit the Tacoma Dome, the world's largest wood dome structure.

796. Visit the Hood Canal Floating Bridge which is the longest floating bridge in the world located in a saltwater tidal basin.

797. Photograph Washington State's Capitol building which was the last state capitol building to be built with a rotunda.

798. Photograph Boeing's Final Assembly Plant, the largest building in the world.

799. Visit the unique Suzzallo Library on the University of Washington campus and learn about its history.

800. Climb to the top of the Volunteer Park Water Tower for a beautiful view of the city.

PHYSICAL CHALLENGES

Another batch of difficult physical challenges, join other Washingtonians in participating in these physical feats.

801. Do the Seattle Rock and Roll Marathon, a running event…with music!

802. Climb Mount Rainier, the highest point in the state of Washington (go with an experienced guide!).

803. Climb the 1,311 stairs to the top of the Columbia Tower.

804. Do the 152-mile RAMROD (Ride Around Mt Rainier in One Day) bicycling event.

805. Do the Bloomsday Run, the premier annual running event in Eastern Washington.

806. Do a triathlon; many are held throughout the state each year.

807. Do a Hash House Harrier run with a Washington Club.

808. Do a Four-Plus Foolhardy Folks extreme volkssporting weekend walking event.

809. Complete the Great Urban Race in Seattle.

810. Participate in the challenging San Juan Island Quest Adventure race.

MARITIME

Being near so much water, a maritime industry is a given. Enjoy these maritime events and places.

811. Go sailing, a popular pastime around the state.

812. Pick up a charter on the Washington coast and go deep-sea fishing.

813. Visit the Olympic Coast Discovery Center in Port Angeles.

814. Visit the historic Westport Maritime Museum and learn about the maritime history of the Washington coast.

815. Visit the interesting Whale Museum at Friday Harbor.

816. Visit the Foss Waterway Seaport and learn about Tacoma's maritime history.

817. Visit the fascinating Feiro Marine Life Center in Port Angeles.

818. Paddle the Cascadia Marine Trail in a non-motorized boat.

819. Visit the small Willapa Seaport Museum.

820. Visit the Coast Guard Museum in Seattle and learn about the history of the Coast Guard in the Pacific Northwest.

HISTORIC BUILDINGS

Although Washington State isn't very old as far as states go, it still has a number of historic buildings.

821. Visit the restored Waterville Historic Hotel, originally built in 1903.

822. Visit the historic Hotel Washington in Chehalis which dates from 1889.

823. Visit the historic Davenport Hotel in Spokane, the first hotel in the United States to have air conditioning.

824. Visit the historic Longmire Buildings located in Mount Rainier National Park.

825. Visit the historic Panama Hotel which features the last remaining Japanese bathhouse in the United States.

1000 Places Washington

826. Visit Officer's Row in Vancouver, part of the Vancouver National Historic Reserve.

827. Photograph the historic Dungeness Schoolhouse near Sequim.

828. Visit the historic town of Oysterville which features many buildings constructed prior to 1880.

829. Visit the Pioneer Building in Seattle, the site of Seattle's first speakeasy during Prohibition.

April Borbon

830. Visit the Meeker Mansion in Puyallup which is listed on the National Register of Historic Places.

MORE GARDENS

With so many beautiful gardens around Washington State we couldn't list just ten so here are ten more to visit.

831. Visit Ohme Gardens which include lush grounds, waterfalls, stone paths, and wonderful views.

Wenatchee [handwritten]

832. Visit the beautiful Lakewold Gardens which includes rare and native plants, trees, rhododendrons, and more.

833. Visit the Bridge of Friendship Japanese Garden in East Wenatchee which celebrates the sister city relationship between East Wenatchee and Misawa Japan.

834. Visit the Finch Arboretum in Spokane which features a "touch and see" nature trail.

835. Visit the Ellensburg Japanese Garden which is located on the campus of Central Washington University.

836. Visit the Bastyr Medicinal Herb Garden which features medicinal herbs, produce used in the school's cafeteria, and a reflexology path (definitely try the reflexology path!).

837. Visit the Highline SeaTac Botanical Garden, created on reclaimed suburban land.

838. Visit the Yakima Area Arboretum which includes a wide array of gardens and displays.

839. Visit the WSU Discovery Garden which features a wide variety of plants and flowers native to the area.

840. Visit the Roozengaarde Display Garden in early spring and see over 300,000 tulips in bloom.

Mount Vernon

WHERE THE HEROES ARE

Every day people are doing heroic things in Washington State. Take a bit of time and go meet some of these heroes.

841. Law enforcement officers risk their lives every day to protect others; take a photo of a law enforcement officer.

842. Firefighters are called on every day to rescue those in danger; take a photo of a fire fighter.

843. Paramedics and EMTs can be the difference between life and death in the field; take a photo of a paramedic or EMT.

844. Washington State is fortunate to have amazingly good medical care; take a photo of a doctor, nurse, or other hospital staff person.

845. Take a photo of a military veteran—there are more than 650,000 living in Washington State. Don't forget to thank them for their service.

846. Take a photo of someone in the Air Force; there are two major Air Force bases located in Washington State.

847. Take a photo of someone in the Army; there are two major Army bases in Washington State.

848. Take a photo of someone in the Navy; there are six naval installations in Washington State.

849. Take a photo of someone in the Marines; there are six naval installations in Washington State which have Marine contingents.

850. Take a photo of someone in the Coast Guard; there are 15 Coast Guard stations in Washington State.

ONLY IN WASHINGTON

Washington does have quite a bit of uniqueness to it. Here are things you will only find in Washington State.

851. Visit Cape Flattery, the northwestern-most point in the Continental United States.

Neah Bay

1000 Places Washington

852. Visit Mineral, the smallest US Post Office in the United States (now closed but still considered the smallest).

853. Visit the Teapot Gas Station in Zillah, the oldest operating gas station in the US.

854. Visit the Hoh, Queets, and Quinault Rain Forests; combined they are the largest temperate rain forest in the United States.

855. Visit the Ice Harbor Lock, the highest single-lift lock in the United States.

April Borbon

856. Visit America's Car Museum in Tacoma, the world's largest private auto collection.

857. Visit the oldest apple tree in the Northwest in Old Apple Tree Park in Vancouver.

858. Visit the totem pole in Kalama, at 140' it is the tallest one-tree totem pole in the world.

859. Visit the Codger Pole, at 65' tall, it is the tallest chainsaw sculpture in the world.

860. Visit the Olympic Sculpture Park, considered a "unique institution' in the United States.

TOURS

Learn even more about various locations in Washington State by taking a guided tour.

861. Take the Seattle Underground Tour and find out why the first level of many downtown Seattle buildings was abandoned.

862. Do the Free Seattle Walking tour (it's a good idea to tip your guide though!).

863. Ride the Duck and tour downtown Seattle and the waterfront.

864. Take the Seattle Chinatown Tour and find out about the history and culture of this unique district.

865. Take a food tour of Pike Place Market; learn about the history and food offerings of this unique market.

866. Take one of the "ghost tours" offered in Washington state and learn about paranormal happenings.

867. Take a cruise tour and tour various areas of the state from the water.

868. Take a food tour of Spokane and learn about the history and food offerings of this city.

869. Take a running tour of Seattle—a unique type of tour that includes…exercise!

870. Do the Seattle Pub Crawl or Coffee Crawl tour.

ALONG THE WATERFRONT

There are a number of beautiful waterfronts to enjoy in Washington State, here are ten to visit.

871. Visit the Seattle waterfront and enjoy the beautiful views of Puget Sound.

872. Walk through Riverfront Park in Spokane which was created for Expo '74.

873. Walk the Columbia River Renaissance Trail and enjoy beautiful views of the Columbia River.

1000 Places Washington

874. Stroll along pretty Bellingham Bay on the South Bay Trail.

875. Walk the Waterfront Loop Trails on Bainbridge Island and enjoy the scenery.

876. Walk the Waterfront Trail in Bremerton and view breakwaters, bridges, boats, and more.

877. Walk the Discovery Trail in Ilwaco and enjoy views of the Pacific Ocean.

878. Walk along the Columbia River waterfront on the Sacagawea Heritage Trail in the Tri Cities.

879. Walk from park to park along the Liberty Bay Trail in Poulsbo.

880. Walk the Tommy Thompson Trail in Anacortes and enjoy views of Birch Bay.

ANNUAL SPORTING EVENTS

Just like other annual events in the state, some people look forward to these annual sporting events all year.

881. Watch the Apple Cup, the annual football rivalry between UW and WSU.

882. Watch the Seafair Hydroplane races, a very popular annual sporting event in Seattle.

883. Attend the Washington Games, an annual sports competition which features 30 different events.

884. Attend the Washington State Senior Games, an annual event which features Olympic-style sporting events for people 50 and older.

885. Watch the world-famous Omak Suicide Race where horses and riders race down Suicide Hill and into the Okanagan River.

886. Watch the Great Prosser Balloon Rally where dozens of hot air balloons take to the skies over Prosser each year.

887. Watch the Washington State Little League Tournament where the best Little League teams in the state compete each year.

888. Watch the Annual Chinese Dragon Boat Races which are part of the Annual Dragon Boat Festival.

889. Watch the annual Seattle Marathon, one of the largest marathon events in the region.

890. Attend the annual Ellensburg Rodeo, one of the top 25 rodeos in the country.

MORE PARKS

Like gardens, there were just too many interesting parks to choose from so here are ten more to visit.

891. Visit Fort Casey State Park which features a sand spit, a lighthouse, a salt water shoreline, and amazing views.

892. Visit Golden Gardens Park, a beachfront park which includes wetlands, sand dunes, and beautiful views.

893. Visit Myrtle Edwards Park which winds around Elliot Bay.

894. Visit Gas Works Park which contains remnants of the only remaining coal gasification plant in the United States.

895. Visit Mt Erie Park and check out the views from the top of the mountain.

anacortes

896. Visit Steamboat Rock State Park which is perched on the edge of Banks Lake.

897. Visit Rockport State Park which features an old-growth forest which has never been logged.

898. Visit Lucia Falls Park located on the East Fork of the Lewis River.

899. Visit the rugged Quillayute River Park.

900. Visit Sun Lake Dry Falls State Park which features Dry Falls, one of the great geological wonders of the United States.

PLACES TO STAY

Enjoy a night or more at these unique places to stay in Washington State.

901. Stay a night at a working dude ranch in Washington State.

902. Stay a night at one of the few five-star hotels in Washington State.

903. Stay at one of the many Bed and Breakfasts located in Washington State.

904. Stay at a hostel in Washington State (except the Green Tortoise Hostel which is its own challenge at #908).

905. Stay a night at one of the few "castles" in Washington State that offer lodging.

906. Stay at the Cedar Creek Treehouses, a unique hotel which has been named one of the world's ten most unusual hotels.

907. Stay at the Lumanaria Sanctuary located in the Columbia River Gorge.

908. Stay at the Green Tortoise Hostel, a storied hostel in downtown Seattle.

909. Stay a night at Our Lady of the Rock Monastery located on Shaw Island.

910. Stay in one of the lighthouses in Washington State that offers lodging.

MUSIC

Even though Seattle is famous for grunge, Washingtonians enjoy a wide range of music. Here are some examples.

911. Visit the Experience Music Project, an interactive museum that focuses on music.

912. Attend a concert at the open-air Gorge Amphitheater.

913. Attend one of the many events at the Icicle Creek Music Center in Leavenworth.

914. Enjoy a community concert, held at community parks and boardwalks throughout the summer around Washington State.

915. Attend a Seattle Musical Theater production.

916. Listen to grunge music in its birthplace—Seattle.

917. Enjoy acoustic music at the Tumbleweed Music Festival in Richland.

918. Attend an event at the Pacific Jazz Institute.

919. Attend the Olympic Music Festival, an annual chamber music festival on the Olympic Peninsula.

920. Enjoy bluegrass music at the Newport Music Festival.

WASHINGTON DAY TRIPS

Washingtonians enjoy easy access to a wide variety of places outside of the state for a day trips.

921. Visit Victoria BC for the day.

922. Take a drive and visit Vancouver BC for the day.

923. Visit Portland, Oregon for the day.

924. Visit Coeur D'Alene, Idaho for the day.

925. Visit the high desert city of Bend, Oregon for the day.

926. Visit the beautiful Oregon Coast for the day.

927. Enjoy a day at Kah Ne Tah in Warm Springs, Oregon for the day.

928. Visit the quaint, seaside town of Astoria, Oregon for the day.

929. Hike to the top of the Multnomah Falls on the Oregon side of the Columbia River Gorge.

930.   Visit Salem, Oregon's capital, for the day.

SOUTHWEST WASHINGTON ATTRACTIONS

Southwest Washington was instrumental in the early history of the state. Here are a number of attractions featured in this section of the state.

931.   Visit Fort Vancouver National Historic Site and learn about the importance of the military and the fur trade to Washington State.

932.   Visit the Pearson Air Museum which includes one of the oldest operating air fields in the nation.

933. Visit the Cedar Creek Grist Mill and take a "working tour" of this historic, water-powered mill.

934. Visit the Cathlapotle Plankhouse, a full-scale replica of a Chinook longhouse in Ridgefield.

935. Visit the Water Resources Education Center and learn about the importance of water resources in the area.

936. Visit Esther Short Park in Vancouver, the oldest public park in the west.

April Borbon

937. Visit Covington House, a historic building that was once a home and a boarding school.

938. Check out the Nutty Narrows Bridge in Longview, a bridge that was built...for squirrels.

939. Walk the Vancouver Land Bridge which connects Fort Vancouver to the Columbia River.

940. Visit Salmon Creek Park, the crown jewel of Vancouver parks.

FUN STUFF

Washington State has a fun side. Here are some examples.

941. Play Pictionary, a game invented in Washington State.

942. Play Pickleball, a game first played in 1965 on Bainbridge Island.

943. Play Cranium, a game invented in Washington State.

944. Do "the wave" at a sporting event (such as at a Huskies game where this crowd sensation was first invented).

April Borbon

945. Take a photo of the Blue Angels as they fly overhead during Seafair.

946. Attend an airshow; there are more than a half dozen of these exciting events held annually around the state.

947. Celebrate Father's Day which was started in Spokane in 1910.

948. Play a Nintendo Game in honor of Redmond being the company's North American headquarters.

949. Listen to a Beatles song (Seattle was the first city in the United States to play a song on the radio from this famous band).

950. Have soft serve ice cream at a Dairy Queen in Olympia (the world's first soft serve ice cream machine was located at a Dairy Queen in Olympia).

REMOTE PLACES

Washington State has some distant places and then there are the remotest and most difficult places to visit. Here are ten to check out.

951. Visit Stehekin, a remote town accessible only by boat, foot, or plane.

952. Visit Gardner Cave, the third longest limestone cave in Washington State located in the extreme northeastern part of the state.

953. Visit Hell's Canyon, North America's deepest river gorge (you will need a boat to access Washington's portion of this canyon).

954. Visit Point Roberts, a town in Washington considered a geopolitical oddity due to the fact that it can only be accessed by air, boat, or by driving through Canada to reach it.

955. Visit the Bodelteh Islands which are considered the western-most point in the 48 contiguous states that are continuously above water (note: they are only accessible by boat!).

956. Drive the Washington portion of the International Selkirk Loop, a highway in the far northeastern part of Washington State.

957. Visit the town of Krupp, also known as Marlin, the smallest incorporated town in Washington State.

958. Visit the Pickett Range, a small range of mountains considered the remotest part of the remote North Cascades mountain range.

959. Visit Holden Village a remote retreat in the mountains above Lake Chelan, accessible by boat.

Holden

960. Visit the Umatilla Reef, located off of Cape Alava and considered the western most point in the 48 contiguous United States, occasionally above water at low tide (you will need a boat for this!).

GHOST TOWNS

Like many places that boomed in the past then dwindled away, Washington State has its share of ghost towns.

961. Visit Anatone, WA, a ghost town which was once an important trading post.

962. Visit what is left of Benge, WA, a once growing railroad town.

963. Visit the remnants of Old Molson, WA, once a mining boomtown.

964. Visit Saint Andrews, WA, once a thriving railroad town.

965. Visit Bordeaux, WA, a once thriving sawmill and logging town.

966. Visit Alstown, WA, an abandoned railroad town in Douglas County.

967. Visit Farmer, WA which includes remnants of a small agricultural community.

1000 Places Washington

968. Visit Lester, WA, a ghost town which was once a railroad and lumber town.

969. Visit Elberton, WA and see what is left of this old sawmill town.

970. Visit Chesaw, WA, an abandoned mining town in Okanagan County.

OLD MINES

First, the disclaimer: be careful! Go as near as safely possibly to the mine and get a photo but don't go into these old abandoned mines which can be extremely dangerous.

971. Visit the Knob Hill Gold Mine which was once the largest producing gold mine in Washington State.

972. Visit the Triple Trip Mine, an abandoned manganese mine in Mason County.

973. Visit the Poland China Mine which was productive from 1896-1939.

974. Visit the Washington Mining and Milling Company mine which is located near the entrance to Mount Rainier Park.

975. Visit the Peshastin Creek Mine, a long abandoned mine in Chelan County.

976. Visit the Antimony Queen Mine which once produced antimony oxide and stibnite ore.

977. Visit the Matwick Mine, an abandoned mine located in Chelan County.

978. Visit the Liberty Mine which is located in an active mining district.

979. Visit the Apex Mine, located in an isolated, mountainous area.

980. Visit the Clipper Mine which is located outside of Tacoma.

MORE HISTORY

We can't forget these historical places that will give you even more insight into the history of Washington State.

981. Visit the Northwest Carriage Museum which features 19th century carriages, buggies, and wagons.

982. Visit the State Capital Museum which is situated in an actual mansion and focuses on the history and culture of Washington State.

983. Visit the city of Aberdeen which has historically been known as the "roughest town west of the Mississippi."

984. Visit the Fort Walla Walla Museum which includes exhibits and a recreated pioneer village.

985. Visit the Columbia River Gorge Interpretive Center Museum which traces the history of the Columbia River Gorge through exhibits, events, and an art gallery.

Stevenson

986. Watch a play at the Kitsap Forest Theater, one of the oldest outdoor theaters in the United States.

Bremerton

987. Visit the Olmstead Place State Park and Museum which includes a working pioneer farm.

988. Visit the Palouse Falls, an amazing falls in Eastern Washington which are both geographically and historically significant.

Franklin Co.

989. Visit the Wing Luke Museum which provides a unique look at the Asian American experience in Washington and in the United States

990. Visit the Northwest African American Museum which focuses on the history and culture of African Americans in the Pacific Northwest.

MORE UNIQUELY WASHINGTON

And finally, even more unique places to check out in Washington State.

991. Eat at Ivar's Acres of Clams which is steeped in Seattle history.

992. Visit Metsker Maps which has been a fixture in Seattle for decades and is beloved by travelers and cartographers alike.

993. Check out Merchants Café which is the oldest existing bar and restaurant in Seattle; it opened in 1890.

994. Take a photo of Seattle's houseboats; Seattle has the largest population of houseboats east of the Orient.

995. Visit one of the many fish hatcheries located in Washington State.

996. Read a book by popular Washington State author Tom Robbins.

997. Visit the Ariel Tavern and Store which pays homage to famed hijacker DB Cooper.

April Borbon

998. Visit the Forks Logging Memorial and Museum which includes a logger's memorial with the names of more than 300 people who have lost their lives to the logging industry.

999. Visit the Hanford Reach National Monument, a protected area which is the US Fish and Wildlife Service's first national monument and the only one within the interior of the United States.

1000. Check out the Washington State Digital Archives, the first-in-the-nation digital archives which preserves state and local documents online.

1000 Places Washington

April Borbon

Index by Number

#	Task	Location
1	Seahawks game	Seattle
2	Mariners game	Seattle
3	WHL Ice Hockey game	varies
4	Seattle Storm game	Seattle
5	Seattle Sounders game	Seattle
6	Minor league baseball game	varies
7	University or college game/sporting event	varies
8	Roller Derby	varies
9	High school game/sporting event	varies
10	Other professional sporting event	varies
11	Debbie Macomber	varies
12	Ann Rule	varies
13	John J. Nance	varies
14	Gregg Olsen	varies
15	Richelle Mead	varies
16	Julia Quinn	varies
17	Steve Martini	varies
18	Elizabeth George	varies
19	Patricia Briggs	varies
20	Lisa Kleypas	varies
21	Kayaking	varies
22	Skiing/snowboarding	varies
23	Fishing	varies
24	Camping	varies
25	Bicycling	varies
26	Shooting	varies
27	Dirt bike/ATV	varies
28	Shell fishing	varies

1000 Places Washington

29	Horseback riding	varies
30	Golf	varies
31	Starvation Heights	Olalla
32	Wah Mee Massacre	Seattle
33	Lakewood Police Massacre	Lakewood
34	Whitman Massacre	Walla Walla
35	Kurt Cobain suicide	Seattle
36	Capitol Hill Massacre	Seattle
37	Centralia Massacre	Centralia
38	Aurora Bridge	Seattle
39	Pang Warehouse Fire	Seattle
40	Roslyn Mining Disaster	Roslyn
41	Bridge of the Gods	North Bonneville
42	Tacoma Narrows Bridge	Tacoma
43	Evergreen Point Floating Bridge	Seattle
44	Covered bridge	varies
45	Deception Pass Bridge	Whidbey Island
46	High Steel Bridge	Mason County
47	Bridge of Glass	Tacoma
48	Interstate Bridge	Vancouver
49	Wishkah River Bridge	Aberdeen
50	Montlake Bridge	Seattle
51	Space Needle	Seattle
52	Pike Place Market	Seattle
53	Columbia Tower	Seattle
54	Fremont Troll	Seattle
55	Chinatown-International District	Seattle
56	Pioneer Square	Seattle
57	Seattle Center/International Fountain	Seattle
58	Smith Tower	Seattle
59	Westlake Center	Seattle

60	Ye Olde Curiosity Shoppe	Seattle
61	Twilight	varies
62	Officer and a Gentleman	varies
63	Sleepless in Seattle	varies
64	Northern Exposure	varies
65	Twin Peaks	varies
66	Disclosure	varies
67	Grey's Anatomy	varies
68	Frasier	varies
69	The Vanishing	varies
70	Free Willy	varies
71	Weyerhaeuser	Federal Way
72	Starbucks	Seattle
73	REI	Seattle
74	Amazon	Seattle
75	Microsoft	Redmond
76	Costco	Seattle
77	Zumiez	Seattle
78	Expedia	Bellevue
79	Jones Soda	Seattle
80	Nordstrom	Seattle
81	Tahoma National Cemetery	Kent
82	Lake View Cemetery	Seattle
83	St Francis Mission Cavalry Cemetery	Toledo
84	Greenwood Memorial Cemetery	Renton
85	Maltby Cemetery	Duval
86	Spokane Falls Cemetery	Spokane
87	Sylvana Graveyard	Sylvana
88	Civil War Cemetery	Seattle
89	Chief Joseph Cemetery	Nespelem
90	Walla Walla State Prison Cemetery	Walla Walla

1000 Places Washington

91	Mount St Helens	Central Cascades
92	Mount Rainier	Central Cascades
93	Mount Baker	North Cascades
94	Mount Adams	Central Cascades
95	Olympic Mountains	Olympic Peninsula
96	Glacier Peak	North Cascades
97	Mount Walker	Quilcene
98	Mount Si	North Bend
99	Desolation Peak	North Cascades
100	Green Mountain	Kitsap County
101	Gingko Petrified Forest	Vantage
102	Cliffside Painted Rocks	Yakima
103	Granite Canyon Rock Art	Omak
104	Marmes Rock Shelter	Franklin County
105	Long Lake Pictographs	Tumtum
106	Petroglyphs at Wedding Rock	Lake Ozette
107	Rock art at Horsethief Lake State Park	Dallesport
108	Ozette Village	Neah Bay
109	Marymoor Prehistoric Indian Site	Redmond
110	Manis Mastodon Site	Sequim
111	Volunteer Park Conservatory	Seattle
112	Hulda Klager Lilac Garden	Woodland
113	Washington Park Arboretum	Seattle
114	Bloedel Reserve	Bainbridge Island
115	Meerkerk Rhododendron Garden	Whidbey Island
116	Kubota Gardens	Seattle
117	Manito Park and Botanical Garden	Spokane
118	Wright Park Arboretum/Seymour Conservatory	Tacoma
119	Rhododendron Species Garden	Federal Way
120	Bellevue Botanical Garden	Bellevue
121	Ride an ugly horse in Wilbur	Wilbur

122	Shuck peanuts on the street in Bremerton	Bremerton
123	Buy a TV on Sunday in Spokane	Spokane
124	Drink and dance at the same time in Lynden	Lynden
125	Walk about in public when you have a cold	All Washington
126	Buy meat on a Sunday	All Washington
127	Pretend that your parents are rich	All Washington
128	Eat a lollipop	All Washington
129	Carry a fishbowl on a Seattle bus	Seattle
130	Destroy another person's beer bottle	All Washington
131	Sol Duc Hot Springs	Olympic Peninsula
132	Bonneville Hot Springs	North Bonneville
133	Carson Hot Springs	Carson
134	Olympic Hot Springs	Olympic Peninsula
135	Baker Hot Springs	Baker Lake
136	Wind River Hot Springs	Stevenson
137	Gamma Hot Springs	Glacier Peak
138	Scenic Hot Springs	Stevens Pass
139	Goldmyer Hot springs	Central Cascades
140	Sulpher Hot Springs	Glacier Peak
141	Cedar Falls	Central Cascades
142	Feature Show Falls	North Cascades
143	Wallace Falls	Central Cascades
144	Otter Falls	King County
145	Twin Falls	North Bend
146	Franklin Falls	Snoqualmie Pass
147	Sol Duc Falls	Olympic Peninsula
148	Marymere Falls	Olympic Peninsula
149	Lower Falls Creek Falls	Carson
150	Ancient Lake waterfalls	Quincy
151	Washington State Capitol Campus	Olympia
152	County courthouse	varies

1000 Places Washington

153	State legislative session	Olympia
154	Join a protest	varies
155	Caucus	varies
156	Meet a state legislator	varies
157	Event at the Capitol Campus	Olympia
158	Washington state flag	varies
159	State flower, state bird, etc.	varies
160	Political rally	varies
161	Chief Timothy State Park	Clarkston
162	Boyer Park	Colfax
163	Lyons Ferry State Park	Franklin
164	Sacajawea State Park	Pasco
165	Horsethief Lake State Park	Dallesport
166	Fort Columbia State Park	Chinook
167	Lewis and Clark Trail State Park	Columbia County
168	Cape Disappointment State Park	Ilwaco
169	Lewis and Clark Memorial Highway	varies
170	Lewis and Clark State Park	Winlock
171	Chateau Ste Michelle Winery	Woodinville
172	Kiona Vineyards and Winery	Benton City
173	Gorman Winery	Woodinville
174	Two Mountain Winery	Zillah
175	Hedges Cellars Winery	Benton City
176	Fidelitas Winery	Benton City
177	Col Solare Winery	Benton City
178	Terra Blanche Winery	Benton City
179	Harbinger Winery	Port Angeles
180	Olympic Cellars Winery	Port Angeles
181	Boundary Bay Brewery	Bellingham
182	Pyramid Brewery	Seattle
183	Elysian Brewing Company	Seattle

184	Redhook Ale Brewery	Woodinville
185	Iron Horse Brewery	Ellensburg
186	Fish Tale Brew Pub	Olympia
187	Pike Brewing Company	Seattle
188	Elliot Bay Brewing Company	Seattle
189	Black Raven Brewing Company	Redmond
190	Icicle Brewing Company	Leavenworth
191	Bainbridge Island	Puget Sound
192	San Juan Island	Strait of Juan de Fuca
193	McNeil Island	Puget Sound
194	Blake Island	Puget Sound
195	Vashon Island	Puget Sound
196	Whidbey Island	Puget Sound
197	Harbor Island	Seattle
198	Lummi Island	Whatcom County
199	Puget Island	Wahkiakum County
200	Protection Island	Strait of Juan de Fuca
201	Lake Crescent	Clallam County
202	Lake Washington	Seattle
203	Vancouver Lake	Vancouver
204	Lake Chelan	Chelan County
205	Lake Sammamish	Issaquah
206	Lake Roosevelt	Grand Coulee
207	Lake Ozette	Clallam County
208	Moses Lake	Grant County
209	Soap Lake	Grant County
210	Spirit Lake	Skamania County
211	Columbia River	varies
212	Yakima River	varies
213	Snake River	varies
214	Wind River	Skamania County

1000 Places Washington

215	White Salmon River	varies
216	Stillaguamish River	varies
217	Sol Duc River	Olympic Peninsula
218	Snoqualmie River	varies
219	Green River	varies
220	Lake Chelan	Chelan County
221	Point No Point Lighthouse	Hansville
222	Cape Flattery Lighthouse	Neah Bay
223	New Dungeness Lighthouse	Clallam County
224	Mukilteo Lighthouse	Mukilteo
225	Alki Point Lighthouse	Seattle
226	Admirality Head Lighthouse	Coupeville
227	Grays Harbor Lighthouse	Westport
228	North Head Lighthouse	Ilwaco
229	Browns Point Lighthouse	Tacoma
230	Cape Disappointment Lighthouse	Ilwaco
231	Highway 101	Olympia-Oregon
232	Chinook Pass Scenic Byway	Sumner-Naches
233	Cascade Loop	North Cascades
234	Olympic Peninsula Loop	Olympic Peninsula
235	Mountain Loop Highway	Snohomish County
236	Spokane River Loop	Spokane
237	Palouse Country Scenic Drive	SE Washington
238	Whidbey Island Scenic Byway	Whidbey Island
239	Chuckanut Drive	Burlington-Bellingham
240	North Pend Oreille Scenic Byway	Tiger-Canada
241	Drive Interstate 5	varies
242	Swim in the Pacific Ocean	varies
243	Visit a ghetto	varies
244	Mt Rainier Lahar area	varies
245	At home	varies

246	Washington mountains	varies
247	Tsunamis	Washington Coast
248	DUI Victim's Panel	varies
249	Earthquake area	varies
250	Wildfire area	varies
251	University of Washington	Seattle
252	Washington State University	Pullman
253	Evergreen State College	Olympia
254	Gonzaga University	Spokane
255	Bastyr University	Kenmore
256	The Art Institute of Seattle	Seattle
257	Cornish College of the Arts	Seattle
258	Seattle University	Seattle
259	State-funded university	various
260	Community College	various
261	Seattle Symphony	Seattle
262	Pacific Northwest Ballet	Seattle
263	Washington Center for the Performing Arts	Olympia
264	Community Theater	varies
265	Seattle Opera	Seattle
266	College or university performing arts	varies
267	Seattle Repertory Theater	Seattle
268	Spokane Symphony	Spokane
269	Performing Arts Center of Wenatchee	Wenatchee
270	Local dance performance	varies
271	Tulalip casino	Tulalip
272	Muckleshoot casino	Auburn
273	LaCenter casino complex	LaCenter
274	Seven Cedars casino	Olympic Peninsula
275	Suquamish Clearwater casino	Suquamish
276	Emerald Queen casino	Tacoma/Fife

1000 Places Washington

277	Snoqualmie casino	Snoqualmie
278	Quinault Casino	Ocean Shores
279	Northern Quest casino	Airway Heights
280	Skagit Valley casino	Bow
281	Outlet mall	varies
282	Ye Olde Curiosity Shoppe	Seattle
283	Nordstrom	Seattle
284	Pike Place Market vendor	Seattle
285	Uwajamaya	Seattle
286	Local shopping mall	varies
287	Amazon.com	online
288	Farmer's market	varies
289	Antique store	varies
290	Locally-owned, non-chain store	varies
291	Seattle Children's Museum	Seattle
292	Children's Museum of Walla Walla	Walla Walla
293	Imagine Children's Museum	Everett
294	Gum Wall at Pike Place Market	Seattle
295	Hands-On Children's Museum	Olympia
296	Soundbridge	Seattle
297	Seattle Children's Film Festival	Seattle
298	Three Rivers Children's Museum	Pasco
299	Rainwall at Westlake Park	Seattle
300	Remlinger Farm	Carnation
301	Boehms Candy Factory tour	Issaquah
302	Seattle Times newspaper factory tour	Bothell
303	Washougal Mill tour	Washougal
304	Darigold Factory tour	Sunnyside
305	Franz Bakery tour	Seattle
306	Liberty Orchards factory tour	Cashmere
307	Boeing Factory Tour	Everett

308	Tsue Chong Fortune Cookie factory tour	Seattle
309	Theo Chocolate Factory tour	Seattle
310	Orondo Cider Works tour	Orondo
311	Washington State History Museum	Tacoma
312	Burke Museum of Natural History and Culture	Seattle
313	Museum of History and Industry	Seattle
314	Whatcom Museum of History and Art	Bellingham
315	Quilcene Historical Museum	Quilcene
316	Clark County Historical Museum	Vancouver
317	Yakima Valley Museum	Yakima
318	History House of Greater Seattle	Seattle
319	Grant County Historical Museum and Village	Ephrata
320	Pomeroy Living History Museum	Yacolt
321	Seattle Art Museum	Seattle
322	Seattle Asian Art Museum	Seattle
323	Museum of Glass	Tacoma
324	Maryhill Museum of Art	Goldendale
325	Henry Art Gallery	Seattle
326	Tacoma Art Museum	Tacoma
327	Museum of Northwest Art	LaConner
328	Frye Art Museum	Seattle
329	Jundt Art Museum	Spokane
330	Northwest Museum of Art and Culture	Spokane
331	Science Fiction Museum and Hall of Fame	Seattle
332	Marvin Carr's One of a Kind in the World Museum	Spokane
333	Marsh's Free Museum	Long Beach
334	Camlann Medieval Village	Carnation
335	Robot Hut Museum	Elk
336	Northwest Museum of Legend and Lore	Seattle
337	Seattle Metropolitan Police Museum	Seattle
338	Washington Banana Museum	online

1000 Places Washington

339	World Kite Museum	Long Beach
340	Rosalie Whyel Museum of Doll Art	Bellevue
341	The Herb Farm Restaurant	Woodinville
342	Space Needle Restaurant	Seattle
343	Dim Sum	Seattle
344	Chef's Kitchen at Inn at Langley	Whidbey Island
345	Ajax Café	Port Hadlock
346	Molly Ward Gardens	Poulsbo
347	Fat Smitty's Café	Discovery Bay
348	Grant House restaurant	Vancouver
349	Dinner cruise	varies
350	Chaco Canyon Café	Seattle
351	Interurban Trail	King County
352	Beacon Rock	South Cascades
353	Clear Creek Trail	Silverdale
354	Hoh Rainforest Trail	Olympic Peninsula
355	Capitol Forest Trail	Olympia
356	Paradise Valley Trail	Snohomish County
357	Spruce Railroad Trail	Olympic Peninsula
358	Point of the Arches Trail	Neah Bay
359	Snoqualmie Falls Trail	Snoqualmie
360	Klickitat Trail	Klickitat County
361	USS Turner Joy	Bremerton
362	Military base	varies
363	Veterans' Memorials	Olympia
364	Naval Undersea Warfare Museum	Keyport
365	Fort Lewis Military Museum	Ft Lewis
366	Puget Sound Navy Museum	Bremerton
367	VFW Hall	varies
368	Eastern Washington State Veteran's Cemetery	Medical Lake
369	State Veteran's Home	varies

April Borbon

370	Veteran's Day Parade	varies
371	Apple	varies
372	Strawberries	varies
373	Cherries	varies
374	Potato	varies
375	Raspberries	varies
376	Grapes	varies
377	Peaches	varies
378	Apricots	varies
379	Pears	varies
380	Hops	varies
381	Wild blackberries	varies
382	Wild huckleberries	varies
383	Wild mushrooms	varies
384	Wild apples	varies
385	Wild greens	varies
386	Wild nuts	varies
387	Truffles	varies
388	Other wild berries	varies
389	Cattails	varies
390	Dumpster diving	varies
391	King County Library (downtown branch)	Seattle
392	Rainier Bank Tower	Seattle
393	Storybook House	Olalla
394	Fort Nisqually	Tacoma
395	Territorial Courthouse	Whatcom County
396	Bigelow House	Olympia
397	Manresa Castle	Port Townsend
398	Troll Haven	Gardiner
399	St John's Cathedral	Spokane
400	Experience Music Project building	Seattle

1000 Places Washington

401	Long Beach	Long Beach
402	Alki Beach	Seattle
403	Deception Pass State Park beach	Whidbey Island
404	Rialto Beach	Olympic Peninsula
405	Dungeness Spit	Olympic Peninsula
406	First, Second, Third beaches	LaPush
407	Obstruction Pass State Park beach	Orcas Island
408	Westport, Grayland, Tokeland beaches	Westport
409	Ediz Hook	Port Angeles
410	Puget Sound/Hood Canal beaches	varies
411	Great Wolf Lodge	Grand Mound
412	Bonneville Hot Springs and Spa	North Bonneville
413	Tulalip Resort and Spa	Tulalip
414	Alderbrook Resort and Spa	Union
415	Semiahmoo Resort and Spa	Blaine
416	Chrysalis Inn and Spa	Bellingham
417	Willows Lodge	Woodinville
418	Salish Lodge and Spa	Snoqualmie
419	Rosario Resort and Spa	Orcas Island
420	Skamania Lodge	Skamania County
421	Geoduck	varies
422	Aplet and Cotlet	varies
423	Salumi cured meats	Seattle
424	Salmon	varies
425	Walla Walla Sweet Onion	varies
426	Venison	varies
427	River trout	varies
428	Chicken Feet	Seattle
429	Cheese	varies
430	Razor clam	varies
431	Bob's Java Jive	Tacoma

April Borbon

432	Toe Truck	Seattle
433	Spite House	Seattle
434	Flower Shop Elephant	Seattle
435	Chiropractic Bigfoot	Federal Way
436	Fremont Rocket	Seattle
437	Bigfoot Statue	Kid Valley
438	World's Largest Egg	Winlock
439	Right-Wing Uncle Sam Billboard	Chehalis
440	Lenin Statue	Seattle
441	Indian Shaker Church	Marysville
442	St Demetrios Greek Orthodox Church	Seattle
443	St James Cathedral	Seattle
444	Claquato Church	Claquato
445	Idriss Mosque	Seattle
446	Overlake Christian Church	Redmond
447	Leavenworth UMC Church	Leavenworth
448	Hindu Temple	Bothell
449	Temple Emanu-El	Spokane
450	Columbia River Washington Temple	Richland
451	Port Townsend	Port Townsend
452	Poulsbo	Poulsbo
453	Leavenworth	Leavenworth
454	Port Gamble	Port Gamble
455	Gig Harbor	Gig Harbor
456	Sequim	Sequim
457	Langley	Langley
458	LaConner	LaConner
459	Winthrop	Winthrop
460	Elbe	Elbe
461	Seattle Pride Parade	Seattle
462	Seattle Torchlight Parade	Seattle

1000 Places Washington

463	Armed Forces Day Parade	Bremerton
464	Fremont Solstice Parade	Seattle
465	Daffodil Festival Grand floral Parade	Pierce County
466	Apple Blossom Festival Parade	Wenatchee
467	Viking Fest Parade	Poulsbo
468	Irrigation Festival Parade	Sequim
469	Selah Days Parade	Selah
470	Woodland Planter's Day Parade	Woodland
471	Woodland Park Zoo	Seattle
472	Olympic Game Farm	Sequim
473	Seattle Aquarium	Seattle
474	Northwest Trek Wildlife Park	Eatonville
475	Point Defiance Zoo and Aquarium	Tacoma
476	Wolf Haven	Tenino
477	Ridgefield National Wildlife Refuge	Ridgefield
478	Umatilla National Wildlife Refuge	Benton County
479	Theler Wetlands	Belfair
480	Cougar Mountain Zoo	Issaquah
481	Northwest Washington Fair	Lynden
482	County Fair	varies
483	Evergreen State Fair	Monroe
484	Puyallup Fair	Puyallup
485	Washington Midsummer Renaissance Fair	Bonney Lake
486	Central Washington State Fair	Yakima
487	Washington State Science and Engineering Fair	varies
488	Washington Civil War Association event	varies
489	Fremont Fair	Seattle
490	Harvest celebration	varies
491	Lavender Festival	Sequim
492	Skagit Valley Tulip Festival	Skagit Valley
493	Washington State International Kite Festival	Long Beach

494	National Lentil Festival	Pullman
495	Model Train Festival	Tacoma
496	Bumbershoot	Seattle
497	Wooden Boat Festival	Seattle
498	Seattle International Film Festival	Seattle
499	Oktoberfest	Leavenworth
500	Northwest Native Arts Market and Festival	Tacoma
501	Coastal webcam	online
502	Bonneville Fishcam	online
503	University webcam	online
504	Mountain webcam	online
505	Ski area cam	online
506	Traffic cam	online
507	Ferry cam	online
508	City cam	online
509	Scenic webcam	online
510	Weather cam	online
511	Weird Washington	varies
512	Snow Falling on Cedars	varies
513	The Egg and I	varies
514	Reservation Blues	varies
515	Breakfast at Sally's	varies
516	Desolation Angels	varies
517	Twilight	varies
518	Ghost Canoe	varies
519	Hotel on the Corner of Bitter and Sweet	varies
520	Drugstore Cowboy	varies
521	Volunteer at a soup kitchen	varies
522	Shop at a thrift store	varies
523	Give out free hugs	varies
524	Volunteer at a community event	varies

1000 Places Washington

525	Do a random act of kindness	varies
526	Donate to a non-profit organization	varies
527	Participate in a charity fundraiser	varies
528	Donate to a food bank	varies
529	Help someone in need	varies
530	Start a Starbucks "cheer chain"	varies
531	Indie band	Seattle
532	Indie newspaper	varies
533	Seattle True Independent Film Festival	Seattle
534	Fremont Vintage Mall	Seattle
535	Vintage clothing store	varies
536	Indie craft fair/market	varies
537	Vintage memorabilia	varies
538	Jack's Country Store	Ocean Park
539	Sasquatch Music Festival	George
540	Indie bookstore	varies
541	Beth's Café	Seattle
542	Drive in movie	varies
543	Dicks Drive In	Seattle
544	Burgerville	varies
545	Mike's Chili Parlor	Ballard
546	Gee Cee's	Toledo
547	Southern Kitchen	Tacoma
548	Voula's Off-Shore Café	Seattle
549	Cougar Country Drive In	Pullman
550	Big Apple Diner	Bremerton
551	Volksmarch	varies
552	HAM Fest	varies
553	Sports club event	varies
554	Book store event	varies
555	Meet up	varies

556	Community garden	varies
557	Community event	varies
558	Kid's sports event	varies
559	Pick-up game of basketball or baseball	varies
560	Support a cause	varies
561	Strip club	varies
562	Emerald Downs	Auburn
563	Sing karaoke	varies
564	Solstice cyclists	Seattle
565	Nude beach	varies
566	Gamble	varies
567	Crash a beach party	varies
568	Rubber Rainbow Condom Company	Seattle
569	Kiss Rachel the Pig	Seattle
570	Center for Sex Positive Culture	Seattle
571	Kenny G	varies
572	Bill Gates	varies
573	Sir Mix a Lot	varies
574	Gary Larson	varies
575	Dale Chihuly	varies
576	Apolo Ohno	varies
577	Kenny Loggins	varies
578	Randy Couture	varies
579	Francis Farmer	varies
580	Bing Crosby	varies
581	DB Cooper	varies
582	Gary Ridgeway	varies
583	Robert Lee Yates	varies
584	Ted Bundy	varies
585	Gypsy Rose Lee	varies
586	Mary Kay Letourneau	varies

587	Greg Nickels	varies
588	Billy Gohl	varies
589	Colton Harris Moore	varies
590	Victor Smith	varies
591	Colville Tribal Museum	Coulee Dam
592	Yakima Nation Museum and Cultural Center	Toppenish
593	Tulalip Tribe's Hilbub Cultural Center	Tulalip
594	Squaxin Tribe Museum	Mason County
595	Makah Cultural and Research Center	Neah Bay
596	Suquamish Tribe Museum	Suquamish
597	Duwamish Tribe's Longhouse and Cultural Center	Seattle
598	Steilacoom Tribal Museum and Cultural Center	Steilacoom
599	Puyallup Tribal Museum	Tacoma
600	Daybreak Star Cultural Center	Seattle
601	Pacific Science Center	Seattle
602	C.R.E.H.S.T.	Richland
603	Hanford B Reactor	Richland
604	Future of Flight Aviation Center	Mukilteo
605	Museum of Flight	Seattle
606	Goldendale Observatory	Goldendale
607	LIGO Hanford Observatory	Richland
608	Jewett Observatory	Pullman
609	Jacobson Observatory	Seattle
610	SPARK Museum	Bellingham
611	Wild Horses Monument	Vantage
612	Fallen Firefighter's Memorial	Seattle
613	Peace Arch	Blaine
614	Maryhill's Stonehenge	Maryhill
615	Gospodor Monuments	Toledo
616	Seattle Fisherman's Memorial	Seattle
617	George Washington Monument	Seattle

April Borbon

618	Bainbridge Island Japanese Exclusion Memorial	Bainbridge Island
619	Anderson Memorial	Spokane
620	Fisherman's Memorial	Bellingham
621	Scottish Highland Games	varies
622	Seafair	Seattle
623	New Years at the Needle	Seattle
624	Seattle Boat Show	Seattle
625	4th of July Fireworks	varies
626	Chinese New Year Celebration	Seattle
627	Christmas Tree Lighting	Leavenworth
628	Seattle Hemp Fest	Seattle
629	Haunted House	varies
630	Christmas Lighted Boat show	varies
631	Festal Event	Seattle
632	Shop in Chinatown	Seattle
633	Dia de los Muertos	varies
634	Great Wall Mall	Kent
635	Halal Market	varies
636	Filipino Restaurant	varies
637	Hispanic music event	varies
638	Pho	varies
639	Indian buffet	varies
640	Russian restaurant	varies
641	Tribal Journeys Canoe event	varies
642	Lelooska Foundation Living History Program	Ariel
643	Tillicum Village	Puget Sound
644	Northwest Indian College	Bellingham
645	Omak Stampede and Pow Wow	Omak
646	Yakima Nation Treaty Days	Yakima
647	Makah Days	Neah Bay
648	Tulalip Annual Veteran's Pow Wow	Tulalip

1000 Places Washington

649	Chief Seattle Days	Suquamish
650	Colville Tribe Annual Pow Wow	Nespelem
651	Olympic National Park	Olympic Peninsula
652	Mount Rainier National Park	Central Cascades
653	North Cascades National Park	North Cascades
654	Mount Baker-Snoqualmie National Forest	Central Cascades
655	Gifford Pinchot National Forest	Southern Cascades
656	Umatilla National Forest	SE Washington
657	Okanogan National Forest	Okanogan County
658	Wenatchee National Forest	Central Cascades
659	Colville National Forest	NE Washington
660	Kaniksu National Forest	NE Washington
661	Cinerama	Seattle
662	Intiman Theater	Seattle
663	Broadway Center for the Performing Arts	Tacoma
664	Capital Playhouse	Olympia
665	Marysville Opera House	Marysville
666	Capitol Theater	Yakima
667	Moore Theater	Seattle
668	Raymond Theater	Raymond
669	Ruby Theater	Chelan
670	Paramount Theater	Seattle
671	Lime Kiln Point State Park	San Juan Island
672	Flaming Geyser State Park	Black Diamond
673	Bridle Trails State Park	Kirkland
674	Dosewallips State Park	Jefferson County
675	Saint Edward State Park	Kenmore
676	Saltwater State Park	Des Moines
677	Lake Wenatchee State Park	Grant County
678	Camano Island State Park	Island County
679	Fay Bainbridge State Park	Bainbridge Island

April Borbon

680	Potholes State Park	Grant County
681	Skydiving	varies
682	SCUBA diving	varies
683	Bungie jumping	varies
684	River rafting	varies
685	Rock climbing	varies
686	Big Four Ice Caves	Granite Falls
687	Ape Cave	Southern Cascades
688	Paintball	varies
689	Mountain climbing	varies
690	Tough man race	varies
691	Top of Beacon Rock	Southern Cascades
692	Puget Sound from Seattle	Seattle
693	Washington Coast	varies
694	Hall of Mosses	Olympic Peninsula
695	Hurricane Ridge	Olympic Peninsula
696	Palouse	Spokane
697	Top of a mountain	varies
698	Channeled Scablands	Lincoln County
699	Fall foliage	varies
700	Mountain	varies
701	Swim in a lake	varies
702	Denny Creek Slide	Central Cascades
703	Edmonds Underwater Park	Edmonds
704	Body surf in the ocean	varies
705	Polar Bear Plunge	varies
706	Swim in a river	varies
707	Waterpark	varies
708	Tidal Pool	varies
709	Windsurfing	varies
710	Swim in the Hood Canal or Puget Sound	varies

1000 Places Washington

711	Dancing	varies
712	Bar	varies
713	Movie	varies
714	Square dancing	varies
715	Attend a rave	varies
716	Comedy Club	varies
717	Live band	varies
718	Midnight movie	varies
719	Billiards	varies
720	Blues or jazz club	varies
721	Queen Anne	Seattle
722	Belltown	Seattle
723	Fremont	Seattle
724	Ballard	Seattle
725	Mercer Island	Seattle
726	Beacon Hill	Seattle
727	South Lake Union	Seattle
728	Wallingford	Seattle
729	Capital Hill	Seattle
730	University District	Seattle
731	Amtrak Coast Starlight	varies
732	Monorail	Seattle
733	Link Lightrail	Seattle
734	Ferry	varies
735	City bus	varies
736	Seaplane	varies
737	Private boat	varies
738	Seattle Sounder train	varies
739	Airplane	varies
740	Canoeing	varies
741	Convention	varies

742	Flashmob	varies
743	Cashmob	varies
744	Wedding	varies
745	Graduation	varies
746	Reddit meet up	varies
747	Barbecue	varies
748	Halloween party	varies
749	Art show/gallery opening	varies
750	Book club meeting	varies
751	Bird watching	varies
752	Rock hounding	varies
753	Fossil hunting	varies
754	Collect seashells	varies
755	Go geocaching	varies
756	Metal detecting	varies
757	Flower pressing	varies
758	Collect leaves	varies
759	Go stargazing	varies
760	Create a scrapbook	varies
761	Starbucks	varies
762	Tully's	varies
763	High Tea	varies
764	Big Foot Java	varies
765	Seattle's Best	varies
766	Bikini Baristas	varies
767	Local, non-chain coffee drive thru	varies
768	Small-batch coffee roaster	varies
769	Seattle Coffee Works tasting room	Seattle
770	Free Coffee Program	varies
771	Crumpet/Crumpet Shop	Seattle
772	Cheese/Beecher Cheese	Seattle

1000 Places Washington

773	Piroshky/Piroshky Piroshky	Seattle
774	Donuts/Daily Dozen Donut Company	Seattle
775	Hom bao/Mee Sum Pastries	Seattle
776	Smoked salmon/Pure Food Fish	Seattle
777	Bread/LePanier	Seattle
778	Tamale/El Puerco Lloron	Seattle
779	Pastry/Three Girls Bakery	Seattle
780	Fish n chips/Jacks Fish Spot	Seattle
781	Pacific Crest Trail	Cascades
782	Mountain to Sound Greenway	Central Cascades
783	John Wayne Pioneer Trail	Eastern Washington
784	Burke Gilman Trail	King County
785	Olympic Discovery Trail	Olympic Peninsula
786	Wonderland Trail	Central Cascades
787	Snoqualmie Valley Regional Trail	King County
788	Centennial Trail	Snohomish County
789	Tolt Pipeline Trail	Central Cascades
790	Snohomish Interurban Trail	Snohomish County
791	Bonneville Dam	North Bonneville
792	Grand Coulee Dam	Grant County
793	Lake Washington Ship Canal/Chittenden Locks	Seattle
794	Union Station	Tacoma
795	Tacoma Dome	Tacoma
796	Hood Canal Floating Bridge	Kitsap County
797	Capitol Building	Olympia
798	Boeing Final Assembly Plant	Everett
799	Suzzallo Library	Seattle
800	Volunteer Park Water Tower	Seattle
801	Seattle Rock and Roll Marathon	Seattle
802	Climb Mount Rainier	Central Cascades
803	Climb Columbia Tower	Seattle

April Borbon

804	Ride RAMROD	Central Cascades
805	Bloomsday Run	Spokane
806	Triathlon	varies
807	Hash House Harrier run	varies
808	Four-Plus Foolhardy Folks volksmarch	varies
809	Great Urban Race	Seattle
810	San Juan Island Quest Adventure Race	San Juan Islands
811	Sailing	varies
812	Deep sea fishing	varies
813	Olympic Coast Discovery Center	Port Angeles
814	Westport Maritime Museum	Westport
815	Whale Museum	San Juan Islands
816	Foss Waterway Seaport	Tacoma
817	Feiro Marine Life Center	Port Angeles
818	Cascadia Marine Trail	Puget Sound
819	Willapa Seaport Museum	Raymond
820	Coast Guard Museum	Seattle
821	Waterville Historic Hotel	Waterville
822	Hotel Washington	Chehalis
823	Davenport Hotel	Spokane
824	Longmire Buildings	Longmire
825	Panama Hotel	Seattle
826	Officer's Row	Vancouver
827	Dungeness School	Sequim
828	Oysterville	Oysterville
829	Pioneer Building	Seattle
830	Meeker Mansion	Puyallup
831	Ohme Gardens	Wenatchee
832	Lakewold Gardens	Lakewood
833	Bridge of Friendship Japanese Garden	East Wenatchee
834	Finch Arboretum	Spokane

835	Ellensburg Japanese Gardens	Ellensburg
836	Bastyr Medicinal Herb Garden	Kenmore
837	Highline SeaTac Botanical Garden	SeaTac
838	Yakima Area Arboretum	Yakima
839	WSU Discovery Garden	Skagit County
840	Roozengaard Display Garden	Mount Vernon
841	Law enforcement officer photo	varies
842	Firefighter photo	varies
843	Paramedic or EMT photo	varies
844	Hospital staffer photo	varies
845	Military veteran photo	varies
846	Air Force personnel photo	varies
847	Army personnel photo	varies
848	Navy personnel photo	varies
849	Marine personnel photo	varies
850	Coast Guard personnel photo	varies
851	Cape Flattery	Neah Bay
852	Mineral Post Office	Mineral
853	Teapot Gas Station	Zillah
854	Hoh, Queets, Quinault Rain Forests	Olympic Peninsula
855	Ice Harbor Lock	Tri Cities
856	America's Car Museum	Tacoma
857	Oldest Apple Tree	Vancouver
858	Totem Pole	Kalama
859	Codger Pole	Colfax
860	Olympic Sculpture Park	Seattle
861	Seattle Underground Tour	Seattle
862	Free Seattle Walking Tour	Seattle
863	Ride the Duck	Seattle
864	Chinatown Tour	Seattle
865	Food tour of Pike Place Market	Seattle

866	Ghost tour	varies
867	Cruise tour	varies
868	Food tour of Spokane	Spokane
869	Running tour	Seattle
870	Pub Crawl/Coffee Crawl	Seattle
871	Seattle Waterfront	Seattle
872	Riverfront Park	Spokane
873	Waterfront Renaissance Trail	Vancouver
874	South Bay Trail	Bellingham
875	Waterfront Loop Trail	Bainbridge Island
876	Waterfront Trail	Bremerton
877	Discovery Trail	Ilwaco
878	Sacagawea Heritage Trail	Tri Cities
879	Liberty Bay waterfront trail	Poulsbo
880	Tommy Thompson Trail	Anacortes
881	Apple Cup	varies
882	Seafair Hydroplane Races	Seattle
883	Washington Games	varies
884	Washington State Senior Games	varies
885	Omak Suicide Race	Omak
886	Great Prosser Balloon Rally	Prosser
887	Washington State Little League Tournament	varies
888	Dragon Boat Races	Seattle
889	Seattle Marathon	Seattle
890	Ellensburg Rodeo	Ellensburg
891	Fort Casey State Park	Whidbey Island
892	Golden Gardens Park	Seattle
893	Myrtle Edwards Park	Seattle
894	Gas Works Park	Seattle
895	Mt Erie Park	Anacortes
896	Steamboat Lake State Park	Electric City

1000 Places Washington

897	Rockport State Park	Rockport
898	Lucia Falls Park	Yacolt
899	Quillayute River Park	Forks
900	Sun Lake Dry Falls State Park	Coulee City
901	Dude Ranch	varies
902	Five-star hotel	varies
903	Bed and Breakfast	varies
904	Youth or Elder hostel	varies
905	Castle	varies
906	Cedar Creek Treehouses	Ashford
907	Luminaria Sanctuary	Stevenson
908	Green Tortoise Hostel	Seattle
909	Our Lady of the Rock Monastery	Shaw Island
910	Lighthouse	varies
911	Experience Music Project	Seattle
912	Gorge Amphitheater concert	George
913	Icicle Creek Music Center	Leavenworth
914	Community concert	varies
915	Seattle Musical Theater	Seattle
916	Grunge music	Seattle
917	Tumbleweed Music Festival	Richland
918	Pacific Jazz Institute	Seattle
919	Olympic Music Festival	Olympic Peninsula
920	Newport Music Festival	Newport
921	Victoria BC	Victoria BC
922	Vancouver BC	Vancouver BC
923	Portland, Oregon	Portland, OR
924	Coeur D'Alene, Idaho	Coeur D'Alene, ID
925	Bend, Oregon	Bend, OR
926	Oregon Coast	varies
927	Kah Ne Tah	Warm Springs, OR

April Borbon

928	Astoria, Oregon	Astoria, OR
929	Multnomah Falls	Troutdale, OR
930	Salem, Oregon	Salem, OR
931	Fort Vancouver National Historic Site	Vancouver
932	Pearson Air Museum	Vancouver
933	Cedar Creek Grist Mill	Washougal
934	Cathlapotle Plankhouse	Ridgefield
935	Water Resources Education Center	Vancouver
936	Esther Short Park	Vancouver
937	Covington House	Vancouver
938	Nutty Narrows Bridge	Longview
939	Vancouver Land Bridge	Vancouver
940	Salmon Creek Park	Vancouver
941	Pictionary	varies
942	Pickleball	varies
943	Cranium	varies
944	The Wave	varies
945	Blue Angels	Seattle
946	Airshow	varies
947	Father's Day	varies
948	Nintendo	varies
949	Beatles Song	varies
950	Soft serve ice cream	Olympia
951	Stehekin	Stehekin
952	Gardner Cave	Pend Oreille County
953	Hell's Canyon	Eastern Washington
954	Point Roberts	Point Roberts
955	Bodelteh Islands	Clallam County
956	International Selkirk Loop	Pend Oreille County
957	Krupp/Marlin	Krupp
958	Picket Range	North Cascades

1000 Places Washington

959	Holden Village	Holden
960	Umatilla Reef	Clallam County
961	Anatone	Asotin County
962	Benge	Adams County
963	Old Molson	Okanogan County
964	Saint Andrews	Douglas County
965	Bordeaux	Thurston County
966	Alstown	Douglas County
967	Farmer	Douglas County
968	Lester	King County
969	Elberton	Whitman County
970	Chesaw	Okanogan County
971	Knob Hill Gold Mine	Ferry County
972	Triple Trip Mine	Mason County
973	Poland China Mine	Okanogan County
974	Washington Milling Company Mine	Pierce County
975	Peshastin Creek Mine	Chelan County
976	Antimony Queen Mine	Okanogan County
977	Matwich Mine	Chelan County
978	Liberty Mine	Kittitas County
979	Apex Mine	King County
980	Clipper Mine	Pierce County
981	Northwest Carriage Museum	Raymond
982	State Capital Museum	Olympia
983	Aberdeen	Aberdeen
984	Fort Walla Walla Museum	Walla Walla
985	Columbia River Gorge Interpretive Center Museum	Stevenson
986	Kitsap Forest Theater	Bremerton
987	Olmstead Place State Park and Museum	Ellensburg
988	Palouse Falls	Franklin County
989	Wing Luke Museum	Seattle

April Borbon

990	Northwest African American Museum	Seattle
991	Ivar's Acres of Clams	Seattle
992	Metsker Maps	Seattle
993	Merchants Café	Seattle
994	Houseboats	Seattle
995	Fish Hatchery	varies
996	Tom Robbins	varies
997	Ariel Tavern and Store	Ariel
998	Forks Logging Museum and Memorial	Forks
999	Hanford Reach National Monument	Eastern Washington
1000	Washington State Digital Archives	online

Index by Location

#	Task	Location
49	Wishkah River Bridge	Aberdeen
983	Aberdeen	Aberdeen
962	Benge	Adams County
279	Northern Quest casino	Airway Heights
125	Walk about in public when you have a cold	All Washington
126	Buy meat on a Sunday	All Washington
127	Pretend that your parents are rich	All Washington
128	Eat a lollipop	All Washington
130	Destroy another person's beer bottle	All Washington
880	Tommy Thompson Trail	Anacortes
895	Mt Erie Park	Anacortes
642	Lelooska Foundation Living History Program	Ariel
997	Ariel Tavern and Store	Ariel
906	Cedar Creek Treehouses	Ashford
961	Anatone	Asotin County
928	Astoria, Oregon	Astoria, OR
272	Muckleshoot casino	Auburn
562	Emerald Downs	Auburn
114	Bloedel Reserve	Bainbridge Island
618	Bainbridge Island Japanese Exclusion Memorial	Bainbridge Island
679	Fay Bainbridge State Park	Bainbridge Island
875	Waterfront Loop Trail	Bainbridge Island
135	Baker Hot Springs	Baker Lake
545	Mike's Chili Parlor	Ballard
479	Theler Wetlands	Belfair
78	Expedia	Bellevue
120	Bellevue Botanical Garden	Bellevue
340	Rosalie Whyel Museum of Doll Art	Bellevue

April Borbon

181	Boundary Bay Brewery	Bellingham
314	Whatcom Museum of History and Art	Bellingham
416	Chrysalis Inn and Spa	Bellingham
610	SPARK Museum	Bellingham
620	Fisherman's Memorial	Bellingham
644	Northwest Indian College	Bellingham
874	South Bay Trail	Bellingham
925	Bend, Oregon	Bend, OR
172	Kiona Vineyards and Winery	Benton City
175	Hedges Cellars Winery	Benton City
176	Fidelitas Winery	Benton City
177	Col Solare Winery	Benton City
178	Terra Blance Winery	Benton City
478	Umatilla National Wildlife Refuge	Benton County
672	Flaming Geyser State Park	Black Diamond
415	Semiahmoo Resort and Spa	Blaine
613	Peace Arch	Blaine
485	Washington Midsummer Renaissance Fair	Bonney Lake
302	Seattle Times newspaper factory tour	Bothell
448	Hindu Temple	Bothell
280	Skagit Valley casino	Bow
122	Shuck peanuts on the street in Bremerton.	Bremerton
361	USS Turner Joy	Bremerton
366	Puget Sound Navy Museum	Bremerton
463	Armed Forces Day Parade	Bremerton
550	Big Apple Diner	Bremerton
876	Waterfront Trail	Bremerton
986	Kitsap Forest Theater	Bremerton
239	Chuckanut Drive	Burlington-Bellingham
300	Remlinger Farm	Carnation
334	Camlann Medieval Village	Carnation

1000 Places Washington

133	Carson Hot Springs	Carson
149	Lower Falls Creek Falls	Carson
781	Pacific Crest Trail	Cascades
306	Liberty Orchards factory tour	Cashmere
91	Mount St Helens	Central Cascades
92	Mount Rainier	Central Cascades
94	Mount Adams	Central Cascades
139	Goldmyer Hot springs	Central Cascades
141	Cedar Falls	Central Cascades
143	Wallace Falls	Central Cascades
652	Mount Rainier National Park	Central Cascades
654	Mount Baker-Snoqualmie National Forest	Central Cascades
658	Wenatchee National Forest	Central Cascades
702	Denny Creek Slide	Central Cascades
782	Mountain to Sound Greenway	Central Cascades
786	Wonderland Trail	Central Cascades
789	Tolt Pipeline Trail	Central Cascades
802	Climb Mount Rainier	Central Cascades
804	Ride RAMROD	Central Cascades
37	Centralia Massacre	Centralia
439	Right-Wing Uncle Sam Billboard	Chehalis
822	Hotel Washington	Chehalis
669	Ruby Theater	Chelan
204	Lake Chelan	Chelan County
220	Lake Chelan	Chelan County
975	Peshastin Creek Mine	Chelan County
977	Matwich Mine	Chelan County
166	Fort Columbia State Park	Chinook
201	Lake Crescent	Clallam County
207	Lake Ozette	Clallam County
223	New Dungeness Lighthouse	Clallam County

955	Bodelteh Islands	Clallam County
960	Umatilla Reef	Clallam County
444	Claquato Church	Claquato
161	Chief Timothy State Park	Clarkston
924	Coeur D'Alene, Idaho	Coeur D'Alene, ID
162	Boyer Park	Colfax
859	Codger Pole	Colfax
167	Lewis and Clark Trail State Park	Columbia County
900	Sun Lake Dry Falls State Park	Coulee City
591	Colville Tribal Museum	Coulee Dam
226	Admirality Head Lighthouse	Coupeville
107	Rock art at Horsethief Lake State Park	Dallesport
165	Horsethief Lake State Park	Dallesport
676	Saltwater State Park	Des Moines
347	Fat Smitty's Café	Discovery Bay
964	Saint Andrews	Douglas County
966	Alstown	Douglas County
967	Farmer	Douglas County
85	Maltby Cemetery	Duval
833	Bridge of Friendship Japanese Garden	East Wenatchee
783	John Wayne Pioneer Trail	Eastern Washington
953	Hell's Canyon	Eastern Washington
999	Hanford Reach National Monument	Eastern Washington
474	Northwest Trek Wildlife Park	Eatonville
703	Edmonds Underwater Park	Edmonds
460	Elbe	Elbe
896	Steamboat Lake State Park	Electric City
335	Robot Hut Museum	Elk
185	Iron Horse Brewery	Ellensburg
835	Ellensburg Japanese Gardens	Ellensburg
890	Ellensburg Rodeo	Ellensburg

1000 Places Washington

987	Olmstead Place State Park and Museum	Ellensburg
319	Grant County Historical Museum and Village	Ephrata
293	Imagine Children's Museum	Everett
307	Boeing Factory Tour	Everett
798	Boeing Final Assembly Plant	Everett
71	Weyerhaeuser	Federal Way
119	Rhododendron Species Garden	Federal Way
435	Chiropractic Bigfoot	Federal Way
971	Knob Hill Gold Mine	Ferry County
899	Quillayute River Park	Forks
998	Forks Logging Museum and Memorial	Forks
163	Lyons Ferry State Park	Franklin
104	Marmes Rock Shelter	Franklin County
988	Palouse Falls	Franklin County
365	Fort Lewis Military Museum	Ft Lewis
398	Troll Haven	Gardiner
539	Sasquatch Music Festival	George
912	Gorge Amphitheater concert	George
455	Gig Harbor	Gig Harbor
137	Gamma Hot Springs	Glacier Peak
140	Sulpher Hot Springs	Glacier Peak
324	Maryhill Museum of Art	Goldendale
606	Goldendale Observatory	Goldendale
206	Lake Roosevelt	Grand Coulee
411	Great Wolf Lodge	Grand Mound
686	Big Four Ice Caves	Granite Falls
208	Moses Lake	Grant County
209	Soap Lake	Grant County
677	Lake Wenatchee State Park	Grant County
680	Potholes State Park	Grant County
792	Grand Coulee Dam	Grant County

221	Point No Point Lighthouse	Hansville
959	Holden Village	Holden
168	Cape Disappointment State Park	Ilwaco
228	North Head Lighthouse	Ilwaco
230	Cape Disappointment Lighthouse	Ilwaco
877	Discovery Trail	Ilwaco
678	Camano Island State Park	Island County
205	Lake Sammamish	Issaquah
301	Boehms Candy Factory tour	Issaquah
480	Cougar Mountain Zoo	Issaquah
674	Dosewallips State Park	Jefferson County
858	Totem Pole	Kalama
255	Bastyr University	Kenmore
675	Saint Edward State Park	Kenmore
836	Bastyr Medicinal Herb Garden	Kenmore
81	Tahoma National Cemetery	Kent
634	Great Wall Mall	Kent
364	Naval Undersea Warfare Museum	Keyport
437	Bigfoot Statue	Kid Valley
144	Otter Falls	King County
351	Interurban Trail	King County
784	Burke Gilman Trail	King County
787	Snoqualmie Valley Regional Trail	King County
968	Lester	King County
979	Apex Mine	King County
673	Bridle Trails State Park	Kirkland
100	Green Mountain	Kitsap County
796	Hood Canal Floating Bridge	Kitsap County
978	Liberty Mine	Kittitas County
360	Klickitat Trail	Klickitat County
957	Krupp/Marlin	Krupp

1000 Places Washington

273	LaCenter casino complex	LaCenter
327	Museum of Northwest Art	LaConner
458	LaConner	LaConner
106	Petroglyphs at Wedding Rock	Lake Ozette
33	Lakewood Police Massacre	Lakewood
832	Lakewold Gardens	Lakewood
457	Langley	Langley
406	First, Second, Third beaches	LaPush
190	Icicle Brewing Company	Leavenworth
447	Leavenworth UMC Church	Leavenworth
453	Leavenworth	Leavenworth
499	Oktoberfest	Leavenworth
627	Christmas Tree Lighting	Leavenworth
913	Icicle Creek Music Center	Leavenworth
698	Channeled Scablands	Lincoln County
333	Marsh's Free Museum	Long Beach
339	World Kite Museum	Long Beach
401	Long Beach	Long Beach
493	Washington State International Kite Festival	Long Beach
824	Longmire Buildings	Longmire
938	Nutty Narrows Bridge	Longview
124	Drink and dance at the same time in Lynden	Lynden
481	Northwest Washington Fair	Lynden
614	Maryhill's Stonehenge	Maryhill
441	Indian Shaker Church	Marysville
665	Marysville Opera House	Marysville
46	High Steel Bridge	Mason County
594	Squaxin Tribe Museum	Mason County
972	Triple Trip Mine	Mason County
368	Eastern Washington State Veteran's Cemetery	Medical Lake
852	Mineral Post Office	Mineral

483	Evergreen State Fair	Monroe
840	Roozengaard Display Garden	Mount Vernon
224	Mukilteo Lighthouse	Mukilteo
604	Future of Flight Aviation Center	Mukilteo
108	Ozette Village	Neah Bay
222	Cape Flattery Lighthouse	Neah Bay
358	Point of the Arches Trail	Neah Bay
595	Makah Cultural and Research Center	Neah Bay
647	Makah Days	Neah Bay
851	Cape Flattery	Neah Bay
89	Chief Joseph Cemetery	Nespelem
650	Colville Tribe Annual Pow Wow	Nespelem
920	Newport Music Festival	Newport
98	Mount Si	North Bend
145	Twin Falls	North Bend
41	Bridge of the Gods	North Bonneville
132	Bonneville Hot Springs	North Bonneville
412	Bonneville Hot Springs and Spa	North Bonneville
791	Bonneville Dam	North Bonneville
93	Mount Baker	North Cascades
96	Glacier Peak	North Cascades
99	Desolation Peak	North Cascades
142	Feature Show Falls	North Cascades
233	Cascade Loop	North Cascades
653	North Cascades National Park	North Cascades
958	Picket Range	North Cascades
659	Colville National Forest	NE Washington
660	Kaniksu National Forest	NE Washington
538	Jack's Country Store	Ocean Park
278	Quinault Casino	Ocean Shores
657	Okanogan National Forest	Okanogan County

1000 Places Washington

963	Old Molson	Okanogan County
970	Chesaw	Okanogan County
973	Poland China Mine	Okanogan County
976	Antimony Queen Mine	Okanogan County
31	Starvation Heights	Olalla
393	Storybook House	Olalla
151	Washington State Capitol Campus	Olympia
153	State legislative session	Olympia
157	Event at the Capitol Campus	Olympia
186	Fish Tale Brew Pub	Olympia
253	Evergreen State College	Olympia
263	Washington Center for the Performing Arts	Olympia
295	Hands-On Children's Museum	Olympia
355	Capitol Forest Trail	Olympia
363	Veterans' Memorials	Olympia
396	Bigelow House	Olympia
664	Capital Playhouse	Olympia
797	Capitol Building	Olympia
950	Soft serve ice cream	Olympia
982	State Capital Museum	Olympia
231	Highway 101	Olympia-Oregon
95	Olympic Mountains	Olympic Peninsula
131	Sol Duc Hot Springs	Olympic Peninsula
134	Olympic Hot Springs	Olympic Peninsula
147	Sol Duc Falls	Olympic Peninsula
148	Marymere Falls	Olympic Peninsula
217	Sol Duc River	Olympic Peninsula
234	Olympic Peninsula Loop	Olympic Peninsula
274	Seven Cedars casino	Olympic Peninsula
354	Hoh Rainforest Trail	Olympic Peninsula
357	Spruce Railroad Trail	Olympic Peninsula

404	Rialto Beach	Olympic Peninsula
405	Dungeness Spit	Olympic Peninsula
651	Olympic National Park	Olympic Peninsula
694	Hall of Mosses	Olympic Peninsula
695	Hurricane Ridge	Olympic Peninsula
785	Olympic Discovery Trail	Olympic Peninsula
854	Hoh, Queets, Quinault Rain Forests	Olympic Peninsula
919	Olympic Music Festival	Olympic Peninsula
103	Granite Canyon Rock Art	Omak
645	Omak Stampede and Pow Wow	Omak
885	Omak Suicide Race	Omak
287	Amazon.com	online
338	Washington Banana Museum	online
501	Coastal webcam	online
502	Bonneville Fishcam	online
503	University webcam	online
504	Mountain webcam	online
505	Ski area cam	online
506	Traffic cam	online
507	Ferry cam	online
508	City cam	online
509	Scenic webcam	online
510	Weather cam	online
1000	Washington State Digital Archives	online
407	Obstruction Pass State Park beach	Orcas Island
419	Rosario Resort and Spa	Orcas Island
310	Orondo Cider Works tour	Orondo
828	Oysterville	Oysterville
164	Sacajawea State Park	Pasco
298	Three Rivers Children's Museum	Pasco
952	Gardner Cave	Pend Oreille County

1000 Places Washington

956	International Selkirk Loop	Pend Oreille County
465	Daffodil Festival Grand floral Parade	Pierce County
974	Washington Milling Company Mine	Pierce County
980	Clipper Mine	Pierce County
954	Point Roberts	Point Roberts
179	Harbinger Winery	Port Angeles
180	Olympic Cellars Winery	Port Angeles
409	Ediz Hook	Port Angeles
813	Olympic Coast Discovery Center	Port Angeles
817	Feiro Marine Life Center	Port Angeles
454	Port Gamble	Port Gamble
345	Ajax Café	Port Hadlock
397	Manresa Castle	Port Townsend
451	Port Townsend	Port Townsend
923	Portland, Oregon	Portland, OR
346	Molly Ward Gardens	Poulsbo
452	Poulsbo	Poulsbo
467	Viking Fest Parade	Poulsbo
879	Liberty Bay waterfront trail	Poulsbo
886	Great Prosser Balloon Rally	Prosser
191	Bainbridge Island	Puget Sound
193	McNeil Island	Puget Sound
194	Blake Island	Puget Sound
195	Vashon Island	Puget Sound
196	Whidbey Island	Puget Sound
643	Tillicum Village	Puget Sound
818	Cascadia Marine Trail	Puget Sound
252	Washington State University	Pullman
494	National Lentil Festival	Pullman
549	Cougar Country Drive In	Pullman
608	Jewett Observatory	Pullman

484	Puyallup Fair	Puyallup
830	Meeker Mansion	Puyallup
97	Mount Walker	Quilcene
315	Quilcene Historical Museum	Quilcene
150	Ancient Lake waterfalls	Quincy
668	Raymond Theater	Raymond
819	Willapa Seaport Museum	Raymond
981	Northwest Carriage Museum	Raymond
75	Microsoft	Redmond
109	Marymoor Prehistoric Indian Site	Redmond
189	Black Raven Brewing Company	Redmond
446	Overlake Christian Church	Redmond
84	Greenwood Memorial Cemetery	Renton
450	Columbia River Washington Temple	Richland
602	C.R.E.H.S.T.	Richland
603	Hanford B Reactor	Richland
607	LIGO Hanford Observatory	Richland
917	Tumbleweed Music Festival	Richland
477	Ridgefield National Wildlife Refuge	Ridgefield
934	Cathlapotle Plankhouse	Ridgefield
897	Rockport State Park	Rockport
40	Roslyn Mining Disaster	Roslyn
930	Salem, Oregon	Salem, OR
671	Lime Kiln Point State Park	San Juan Island
810	San Juan Island Quest Adventure Race	San Juan Islands
815	Whale Museum	San Juan Islands
837	Highline SeaTac Botanical Garden	SeaTac
871	Seattle Waterfront	Seattle
1	Seahawks game	Seattle
2	Mariners game	Seattle
4	Seattle Storm game	Seattle

1000 Places Washington

5	Seattle Sounders game	Seattle
32	Wah Mee Massacre	Seattle
35	Kurt Cobain suicide	Seattle
36	Capitol Hill Massacre	Seattle
38	Aurora Bridge	Seattle
39	Pang Warehouse Fire	Seattle
43	Evergreen Point Floating Bridge	Seattle
50	Montlake Bridge	Seattle
51	Space Needle	Seattle
52	Pike Place Market	Seattle
53	Columbia Tower	Seattle
54	Fremont Troll	Seattle
55	Chinatown-International District	Seattle
56	Pioneer Square	Seattle
57	Seattle Center/International Fountain	Seattle
58	Smith Tower	Seattle
59	Westlake Center	Seattle
60	Ye Olde Curiosity Shoppe	Seattle
72	Starbucks	Seattle
73	REI	Seattle
74	Amazon	Seattle
76	Costco	Seattle
77	Zumiez	Seattle
79	Jones Soda	Seattle
80	Nordstrom	Seattle
82	Lake View Cemetery	Seattle
88	Civil War Cemetery	Seattle
111	Volunteer Park Conservatory	Seattle
113	Washington Park Arboretum	Seattle
116	Kubota Gardens	Seattle
129	Fishbowl on a bus in Seattle	Seattle

182	Pyramid Brewery	Seattle
183	Elysian Brewing Company	Seattle
187	Pike Brewing Company	Seattle
188	Elliot Bay Brewing Company	Seattle
197	Harbor Island	Seattle
202	Lake Washington	Seattle
225	Alki Point Lighthouse	Seattle
251	University of Washington	Seattle
256	The Art Institute of Seattle	Seattle
257	Cornish College of the Arts	Seattle
258	Seattle University	Seattle
261	Seattle Symphony	Seattle
262	Pacific Northwest Ballet	Seattle
265	Seattle Opera	Seattle
267	Seattle Repertory Theater	Seattle
282	Ye Olde Curiosity Shoppe	Seattle
283	Nordstrom	Seattle
284	Pike Place Market vendor	Seattle
285	Uwajamaya	Seattle
291	Seattle Children's Museum	Seattle
294	Gum Wall at Pike Place Market	Seattle
296	Soundbridge	Seattle
297	Seattle Children's Film Festival	Seattle
299	Rainwall at Westlake Park	Seattle
305	Franz Bakery tour	Seattle
308	Tsue Chong Fortune Cookie factory tour	Seattle
309	Theo Chocolate Factory tour	Seattle
312	Burke Museum of Natural History and Culture	Seattle
313	Museum of History and Industry	Seattle
318	History House of Greater Seattle	Seattle
321	Seattle Art Museum	Seattle

1000 Places Washington

322	Seattle Asian Art Museum	Seattle
325	Henry Art Gallery	Seattle
328	Frye Art Museum	Seattle
331	Science Fiction Museum and Hall of Fame	Seattle
336	Northwest Museum of Legend and Lore	Seattle
337	Seattle Metropolitan Police Museum	Seattle
342	Space Needle Restaurant	Seattle
343	Dim Sum	Seattle
350	Chaco Canyon Café	Seattle
391	King County Library (downtown branch)	Seattle
392	Rainier Bank Tower	Seattle
400	Experience Music Project building	Seattle
402	Alki Beach	Seattle
423	Salumi cured meats	Seattle
428	Chicken Feet	Seattle
432	Toe Truck	Seattle
433	Spite House	Seattle
434	Flower Shop Elephant	Seattle
436	Fremont Rocket	Seattle
440	Lenin Statue	Seattle
442	St Demetrios Greek Orthodox Church	Seattle
443	St James Cathedral	Seattle
445	Idriss Mosque	Seattle
461	Seattle Pride Parade	Seattle
462	Seattle Torchlight Parade	Seattle
464	Fremont Solstice Parade	Seattle
471	Woodland Park Zoo	Seattle
473	Seattle Aquarium	Seattle
489	Fremont Fair	Seattle
496	Bumbershoot	Seattle
497	Wooden Boat Festival	Seattle

498	Seattle International Film Festival	Seattle
531	Indie band	Seattle
533	Seattle True Independent Film Festival	Seattle
534	Fremont Vintage Mall	Seattle
541	Beth's Café	Seattle
543	Dicks Drive In	Seattle
548	Voula's Off-Shore Café	Seattle
564	Solstice cyclists	Seattle
568	Rubber Rainbow Condom Company	Seattle
569	Kiss Rachel the Pig	Seattle
570	Center for Sex Positive Culture	Seattle
597	Duwamish Tribe's Longhouse and Cultural Center	Seattle
600	Daybreak Star Cultural Center	Seattle
601	Pacific Science Center	Seattle
605	Museum of Flight	Seattle
609	Jacobson Observatory	Seattle
612	Fallen Firefighter's Memorial	Seattle
616	Seattle Fisherman's Memorial	Seattle
617	George Washington Monument	Seattle
622	Seafair	Seattle
623	New Years at the Needle	Seattle
624	Seattle Boat Show	Seattle
626	Chinese New Year Celebration	Seattle
628	Seattle Hemp Fest	Seattle
631	Festal Event	Seattle
632	Shop in Chinatown	Seattle
661	Cinerama	Seattle
662	Intiman Theater	Seattle
667	Moore Theater	Seattle
670	Paramount Theater	Seattle
692	Puget Sound from Seattle	Seattle

1000 Places Washington

721	Queen Anne	Seattle
722	Belltown	Seattle
723	Fremont	Seattle
724	Ballard	Seattle
725	Mercer Island	Seattle
726	Beacon Hill	Seattle
727	South Lake Union	Seattle
728	Wallingford	Seattle
729	Capital Hill	Seattle
730	University District	Seattle
732	Monorail	Seattle
733	Link Lightrail	Seattle
769	Seattle Coffee Works tasting room	Seattle
771	Crumpet/Crumpet Shop	Seattle
772	Cheese/Beecher Cheese	Seattle
773	Piroshky/Piroshky Piroshky	Seattle
774	Donuts/Daily Dozen Donut Company	Seattle
775	Hom bao/Mee Sum Pastries	Seattle
776	Smoked salmon/Pure Food Fish	Seattle
777	Bread/LePanier	Seattle
778	Tamale/El Puerco Lloron	Seattle
779	Pastry/Three Girls Bakery	Seattle
780	Fish n chips/Jacks Fish Spot	Seattle
793	Lake Washington Ship Canal/Chittenden Locks	Seattle
799	Suzzallo Library	Seattle
800	Volunteer Park Water Tower	Seattle
801	Seattle Rock and Roll Marathon	Seattle
803	Climb Columbia Tower	Seattle
809	Great Urban Race	Seattle
820	Coast Guard Museum	Seattle
825	Panama Hotel	Seattle

829	Pioneer Building	Seattle
860	Olympic Sculpture Park	Seattle
861	Seattle Underground Tour	Seattle
862	Free Seattle Walking Tour	Seattle
863	Ride the Duck	Seattle
864	Chinatown Tour	Seattle
865	Food tour of Pike Place Market	Seattle
869	Running tour	Seattle
870	Pub Crawl/Coffee Crawl	Seattle
882	Seafair Hydroplane Races	Seattle
888	Dragon Boat Races	Seattle
889	Seattle Marathon	Seattle
892	Golden Gardens Park	Seattle
893	Myrtle Edwards Park	Seattle
894	Gas Works Park	Seattle
908	Green Tortoise Hostel	Seattle
911	Experience Music Project	Seattle
915	Seattle Musical Theater	Seattle
916	Grunge music	Seattle
918	Pacific Jazz Institute	Seattle
945	Blue Angels	Seattle
989	Wing Luke Museum	Seattle
990	Northwest African American Museum	Seattle
991	Ivar's Acres of Clams	Seattle
992	Metsker Maps	Seattle
993	Merchants Café	Seattle
994	Houseboats	Seattle
469	Selah Days Parade	Selah
110	Manis Mastodon Site	Sequim
456	Sequim	Sequim
468	Irrigation Festival Parade	Sequim

1000 Places Washington

472	Olympic Game Farm	Sequim
491	Lavender Festival	Sequim
827	Dungeness School	Sequim
909	Our Lady of the Rock Monastery	Shaw Island
353	Clear Creek Trail	Silverdale
839	WSU Discovery Garden	Skagit County
492	Skagit Valley Tulip Festival	Skagit Valley
210	Spirit Lake	Skamania County
214	Wind River	Skamania County
420	Skamania Lodge	Skamania County
235	Mountain Loop Highway	Snohomish County
356	Paradise Valley Trail	Snohomish County
788	Centennial Trail	Snohomish County
790	Snohomish Interurban Trail	Snohomish County
277	Snoqualmie casino	Snoqualmie
359	Snoqualmie Falls Trail	Snoqualmie
418	Salish Lodge and Spa	Snoqualmie
146	Franklin Falls	Snoqualmie Pass
352	Beacon Rock	South Cascades
656	Umatilla National Forest	SE Washington
237	Palouse Country Scenic Drive	SE Washington
655	Gifford Pinchot National Forest	Southern Cascades
687	Ape Cave	Southern Cascades
691	Top of Beacon Rock	Southern Cascades
86	Spokane Falls Cemetery	Spokane
117	Manito Park and Botanical Garden	Spokane
123	Buy a TV on Sunday in Spokane	Spokane
236	Spokane River Loop	Spokane
254	Gonzaga University	Spokane
268	Spokane Symphony	Spokane
329	Jundt Art Museum	Spokane

330	Northwest Museum of Art and Culture	Spokane
332	Marvin Carr's One of a Kind in the World Museum	Spokane
399	St John's Cathedral	Spokane
449	Temple Emanu-El	Spokane
619	Anderson Memorial	Spokane
696	Palouse	Spokane
805	Bloomsday Run	Spokane
823	Davenport Hotel	Spokane
834	Finch Arboretum	Spokane
868	Food tour of Spokane	Spokane
872	Riverfront Park	Spokane
951	Stehekin	Stehekin
598	Steilacoom Tribal Museum and Cultural Center	Steilacoom
138	Scenic Hot Springs	Stevens Pass
136	Wind River Hot Springs	Stevenson
907	Luminaria Sanctuary	Stevenson
985	Columbia River Gorge Interpretive Center Museum	Stevenson
192	San Juan Island	Strait of Juan de Fuca
200	Protection Island	Strait of Juan de Fuca
232	Chinook Pass Scenic Byway	Sumner-Naches
304	Darigold Factory tour	Sunnyside
275	Suquamish Clearwater casino	Suquamish
596	Suquamish Tribe Museum	Suquamish
649	Chief Seattle Days	Suquamish
87	Sylvana Graveyard	Sylvana
42	Tacoma Narrows Bridge	Tacoma
47	Bridge of Glass	Tacoma
118	Wright Park Arboretum/Seymour Conservatory	Tacoma
229	Browns Point Lighthouse	Tacoma
311	Washington State History Museum	Tacoma
323	Museum of Glass	Tacoma

1000 Places Washington

326	Tacoma Art Museum	Tacoma
394	Fort Nisqually	Tacoma
431	Bob's Java Jive	Tacoma
475	Point Defiance Zoo and Aquarium	Tacoma
495	Model Train Festival	Tacoma
500	Northwest Native Arts Market and Festival	Tacoma
547	Southern Kitchen	Tacoma
599	Puyallup Tribal Museum	Tacoma
663	Broadway Center for the Performing Arts	Tacoma
794	Union Station	Tacoma
795	Tacoma Dome	Tacoma
816	Foss Waterway Seaport	Tacoma
856	America's Car Museum	Tacoma
276	Emerald Queen casino	Tacoma/Fife
476	Wolf Haven	Tenino
965	Bordeaux	Thurston County
240	North Pend Oreille Scenic Byway	Tiger-Canada
83	St Francis Mission Cavalry Cemetery	Toledo
546	Gee Cee's	Toledo
615	Gospodor Monuments	Toledo
592	Yakima Nation Museum and Cultural Center	Toppenish
855	Ice Harbor Lock	Tri Cities
878	Sacagawea Heritage Trail	Tri Cities
929	Multnomah Falls	Troutdale, OR
271	Tulalip casino	Tulalip
413	Tulalip Resort and Spa	Tulalip
593	Tulalip Tribe's Hilbub Cultural Center	Tulalip
648	Tulalip Annual Veteran's Pow Wow	Tulalip
105	Long Lake Pictographs	Tumtum
414	Alderbrook Resort and Spa	Union
48	Interstate Bridge	Vancouver

April Borbon

203	Vancouver Lake	Vancouver
316	Clark County Historical Museum	Vancouver
348	Grant House restaurant	Vancouver
826	Officer's Row	Vancouver
857	Oldest Apple Tree	Vancouver
873	Waterfront Renaissance Trail	Vancouver
931	Fort Vancouver National Historic Site	Vancouver
932	Pearson Air Museum	Vancouver
935	Water Resources Education Center	Vancouver
936	Esther Short Park	Vancouver
937	Covington House	Vancouver
939	Vancouver Land Bridge	Vancouver
940	Salmon Creek Park	Vancouver
922	Vancouver BC	Vancouver BC
101	Gingko Petrified Forest	Vantage
611	Wild Horses Monument	Vantage
3	WHL Ice Hockey game	varies
6	Minor league baseball game	varies
7	University or college game/sporting event	varies
8	Roller Derby	varies
9	High school game/sporting event	varies
10	Other professional sporting event	varies
11	Debbie Macomber	varies
12	Ann Rule	varies
13	John J. Nance	varies
14	Gregg Olsen	varies
15	Richelle Mead	varies
16	Julia Quinn	varies
17	Steve Martini	varies
18	Elizabeth George	varies
19	Patricia Briggs	varies

1000 Places Washington

20	Lisa Kleypas	varies
21	Kayaking	varies
22	Skiing/snowboarding	varies
23	Fishing	varies
24	Camping	varies
25	Bicycling	varies
26	Shooting	varies
27	Dirt bike/ATV	varies
28	Shell fishing	varies
29	Horseback riding	varies
30	Golf	varies
44	Covered bridge	varies
61	Twilight	varies
62	Officer and a Gentleman	varies
63	Sleepless in Seattle	varies
64	Northern Exposure	varies
65	Twin Peaks	varies
66	Disclosure	varies
67	Grey's Anatomy	varies
68	Frasier	varies
69	The Vanishing	varies
70	Free Willy	varies
152	County courthouse	varies
154	Join a protest	varies
155	Caucus	varies
156	Meet a state legislator	varies
158	Washington state flag	varies
159	State flower, state bird, etc.	varies
160	Political rally	varies
169	Lewis and Clark Memorial Highway	varies
211	Columbia River	varies

212	Yakima River	varies
213	Snake River	varies
215	White Salmon River	varies
216	Stillaguamish River	varies
218	Snoqualmie River	varies
219	Green River	varies
241	Drive Interstate 5	varies
242	Swim in the Pacific Ocean	varies
243	Visit a ghetto	varies
244	Mt Rainier Lahar area	varies
245	At home	varies
246	Washington mountains	varies
248	DUI Victim's Panel	varies
249	Earthquake area	varies
250	Wildfire area	varies
264	Community Theater	varies
266	College or university performing arts	varies
270	Local dance performance	varies
281	Outlet mall	varies
286	Local shopping mall	varies
288	Farmer's market	varies
289	Antique store	varies
290	Locally-owned, non-chain store	varies
349	Dinner cruise	varies
362	Military base	varies
367	VFW Hall	varies
369	State Veteran's Home	varies
370	Veteran's Day Parade	varies
371	Apple	varies
372	Strawberries	varies
373	Cherries	varies

1000 Places Washington

374	Potato	varies
375	Raspberries	varies
376	Grapes	varies
377	Peaches	varies
378	Apricots	varies
379	Pears	varies
380	Hops	varies
381	Wild blackberries	varies
382	Wild huckleberries	varies
383	Wild mushrooms	varies
384	Wild apples	varies
385	Wild greens	varies
386	Wild nuts	varies
387	Truffles	varies
388	Other wild berries	varies
389	Cattails	varies
390	Dumpster diving	varies
410	Puget Sound/Hood Canal beaches	varies
421	Geoduck	varies
422	Aplet and Cotlet	varies
424	Salmon	varies
425	Walla Walla Sweet Onion	varies
426	Venison	varies
427	River trout	varies
429	Cheese	varies
430	Razor clam	varies
482	County Fair	varies
487	Washington State Science and Engineering Fair	varies
488	Washington Civil War Association event	varies
490	Harvest celebration	varies
511	Weird Washington	varies

512	Snow Falling on Cedars	varies
513	The Egg and I	varies
514	Reservation Blues	varies
515	Breakfast at Sally's	varies
516	Desolation Angels	varies
517	Twilight	varies
518	Ghost Canoe	varies
519	Hotel on the Corner of Bitter and Sweet	varies
520	Drugstore Cowboy	varies
521	Volunteer at a soup kitchen	varies
522	Shop at a thrift store	varies
523	Give out free hugs	varies
524	Volunteer at a community event	varies
525	Do a random act of kindness	varies
526	Donate to a non-profit organization	varies
527	Participate in a charity fundraiser	varies
528	Donate to a food bank	varies
529	Help someone in need	varies
530	Start a Starbucks "cheer chain"	varies
532	Indie newspaper	varies
535	Vintage clothing store	varies
536	Indie craft fair/market	varies
537	Vintage memorabilia	varies
540	Indie bookstore	varies
542	Drive in movie	varies
544	Burgerville	varies
551	Volksmarch	varies
552	HAM Fest	varies
553	Sports club event	varies
554	Book store event	varies
555	Meet up	varies

1000 Places Washington

556	Community garden	varies
557	Community event	varies
558	Kid's sports event	varies
559	Pick-up game of basketball or baseball	varies
560	Support a cause	varies
561	Strip club	varies
563	Sing karaoke	varies
565	Nude beach	varies
566	Gamble	varies
567	Crash a beach party	varies
571	Kenny G	varies
572	Bill Gates	varies
573	Sir Mix a Lot	varies
574	Gary Larson	varies
575	Dale Chihuly	varies
576	Apolo Ohno	varies
577	Kenny Loggins	varies
578	Randy Couture	varies
579	Francis Farmer	varies
580	Bing Crosby	varies
581	DB Cooper	varies
582	Gary Ridgeway	varies
583	Robert Lee Yates	varies
584	Ted Bundy	varies
585	Gypsy Rose Lee	varies
586	Mary Kay Letourneau	varies
587	Greg Nickels	varies
588	Billy Gohl	varies
589	Colton Harris Moore	varies
590	Victor Smith	varies
621	Scottish Highland Games	varies

625	4th of July Fireworks	varies
629	Haunted House	varies
630	Christmas Lighted Boat show	varies
633	Dia de los Muertos	varies
635	Halal Market	varies
636	Filipino Restaurant	varies
637	Hispanic music event	varies
638	Pho	varies
639	Indian buffet	varies
640	Russian restaurant	varies
641	Tribal Journeys Canoe event	varies
681	Skydiving	varies
682	SCUBA diving	varies
683	Bungie jumping	varies
684	River rafting	varies
685	Rock climbing	varies
688	Paintball	varies
689	Mountain climbing	varies
690	Tough man race	varies
693	Washington Coast	varies
697	Top of a mountain	varies
699	Fall foliage	varies
700	Mountain	varies
701	Swim in a lake	varies
704	Body surf in the ocean	varies
705	Polar Bear Plunge	varies
706	Swim in a river	varies
707	Waterpark	varies
708	Tidal Pool	varies
709	Windsurfing	varies
710	Swim in the Hood Canal or Puget Sound	varies

1000 Places Washington

711	Dancing	varies
712	Bar	varies
713	Movie	varies
714	Square dancing	varies
715	Attend a rave	varies
716	Comedy Club	varies
717	Live band	varies
718	Midnight movie	varies
719	Billiards	varies
720	Blues or jazz club	varies
731	Amtrak Coast Starlight	varies
734	Ferry	varies
735	City bus	varies
736	Seaplane	varies
737	Private boat	varies
738	Seattle Sounder train	varies
739	Airplane	varies
740	Canoeing	varies
741	Convention	varies
742	Flashmob	varies
743	Cashmob	varies
744	Wedding	varies
745	Graduation	varies
746	Reddit meet up	varies
747	Barbecue	varies
748	Halloween party	varies
749	Art show/gallery opening	varies
750	Book club meeting	varies
751	Bird watching	varies
752	Rock hounding	varies
753	Fossil hunting	varies

April Borbon

754	Collect seashells	varies
755	Go geocaching	varies
756	Metal detecting	varies
757	Flower pressing	varies
758	Collect leaves	varies
759	Go stargazing	varies
760	Create a scrapbook	varies
761	Starbucks	varies
762	Tully's	varies
763	High Tea	varies
764	Big Foot Java	varies
765	Seattle's Best	varies
766	Bikini Baristas	varies
767	Local, non-chain coffee drive thru	varies
768	Small-batch coffee roaster	varies
770	Free Coffee Program	varies
806	Triathlon	varies
807	Hash House Harrier run	varies
808	Four-Plus Foolhardy Folks volksmarch	varies
811	Sailing	varies
812	Deep sea fishing	varies
841	Law enforcement officer photo	varies
842	Firefighter photo	varies
843	Paramedic or EMT photo	varies
844	Hospital staffer photo	varies
845	Military veteran photo	varies
846	Air Force personnel photo	varies
847	Army personnel photo	varies
848	Navy personnel photo	varies
849	Marine personnel photo	varies
850	Coast Guard personnel photo	varies

866	Ghost tour	varies
867	Cruise tour	varies
881	Apple Cup	varies
883	Washington Games	varies
884	Washington State Senior Games	varies
887	Washington State Little League Tournament	varies
901	Dude Ranch	varies
902	Five-star hotel	varies
903	Bed and Breakfast	varies
904	Youth or Elder hostel	varies
905	Castle	varies
910	Lighthouse	varies
914	Community concert	varies
926	Oregon Coast	varies
941	Pictionary	varies
942	Pickleball	varies
943	Cranium	varies
944	The Wave	varies
946	Airshow	varies
947	Father's Day	varies
948	Nintendo	varies
949	Beatles Song	varies
995	Fish Hatchery	varies
996	Tom Robbins	varies
259	State-funded university	various
260	Community College	various
921	Victoria BC	Victoria BC
199	Puget Island	Wahkiakum County
34	Whitman Massacre	Walla Walla
90	Walla Walla State Prison Cemetery	Walla Walla
292	Children's Museum of Walla Walla	Walla Walla

April Borbon

984	Fort Walla Walla Museum	Walla Walla
927	Kah Ne Tah	Warm Springs, OR
247	Tsunamis	Washington Coast
303	Washougal Mill tour	Washougal
933	Cedar Creek Grist Mill	Washougal
821	Waterville Historic Hotel	Waterville
269	Performing Arts Center of Wenatchee	Wenatchee
466	Apple Blossom Festival Parade	Wenatchee
831	Ohme Gardens	Wenatchee
227	Grays Harbor Lighthouse	Westport
408	Westport, Grayland, Tokeland beaches	Westport
814	Westport Maritime Museum	Westport
198	Lummi Island	Whatcom County
395	Territorial Courthouse	Whatcom County
45	Deception Pass Bridge	Whidbey Island
115	Meerkerk Rhododendron Garden	Whidbey Island
238	Whidbey Island Scenic Byway	Whidbey Island
344	Chef's Kitchen at Inn at Langley	Whidbey Island
403	Deception Pass State Park beach	Whidbey Island
891	Fort Casey State Park	Whidbey Island
969	Elberton	Whitman County
121	Ride an ugly horse in Wilbur	Wilbur
170	Lewis and Clark State Park	Winlock
438	World's Largest Egg	Winlock
459	Winthrop	Winthrop
171	Chateau Ste Michelle Winery	Woodinville
173	Gorman Winery	Woodinville
184	Redhook Ale Brewery	Woodinville
341	The Herb Farm Restaurant	Woodinville
417	Willows Lodge	Woodinville
112	Hulda Klager Lilac Garden	Woodland

1000 Places Washington

470	Woodland Planter's Day Parade	Woodland
320	Pomeroy Living History Museum	Yacolt
898	Lucia Falls Park	Yacolt
102	Cliffside Painted Rocks	Yakima
317	Yakima Valley Museum	Yakima
486	Central Washington State Fair	Yakima
646	Yakima Nation Treaty Days	Yakima
666	Capitol Theater	Yakima
838	Yakima Area Arboretum	Yakima
174	Two Mountain Winery	Zillah
853	Teapot Gas Station	Zillah

ABOUT THE AUTHOR

April Borbon is a freelance writer, traveler, and business consultant who was born and raised in Washington State.

Made in the USA
Lexington, KY
06 December 2012